Rockhounding For Total Beginners

Emme .X Dawson

Introduction

This is a comprehensive guide tailored to beginners eager to embark on the captivating journey of rock and mineral collection. It not only introduces readers to the basics of rockhounding but also delves into the rich historical context of this timeless hobby, highlighting its ancient origins and modern-day significance.

The guide goes on to explain the practical aspects of rockhounding, equipping enthusiasts with the essential knowledge required to get started.

One of the key aspects covered is the equipment and tools necessary for successful rockhounding expeditions, ensuring that beginners are well-prepared to explore the world of geological wonders. Additionally, the guide emphasizes the importance of understanding the legal regulations and ethical considerations surrounding rock collecting, ensuring that enthusiasts engage responsibly.

Readers are also provided with valuable insights into where to search for rocks, minerals, geodes, and fossils, guiding them to promising locations both domestically and internationally. The guide takes them step-by-step through the process of starting and organizing a rock collection, offering practical advice on preserving and showcasing their treasures.

An essential skill for rockhounds is the ability to identify various rocks and minerals, and this guide dedicates a section to honing this skill. It also introduces readers to the most significant rocks and minerals to seek out during their rockhounding adventures, including some of the most valuable gemstones in the world.

For those looking to turn their passion into profit, the guide explores avenues for making money through rocks, whether it's selling collections, running a rock-related business, or utilizing social media and online platforms. It even delves into the realm of jewelry-making, offering insights into starting an online jewelry business using rocks, minerals, and gems.

In essence, this book serves as a comprehensive resource that equips beginners with the knowledge, skills, and guidance needed to embark on a rewarding and fulfilling journey in the world of rock and mineral collection, all while emphasizing responsible and ethical rockhounding practices.

Contents

Book 1
Rockhounding Basics

Introduction

Lots of people are collecting things. Interest in collecting objects appears from an early age. For example, collecting coins, books, stamps, and stones is of interest to adults and growing children. Over the years, many lose interest and leave this occupation, but the most avid collectors turn their hobby into professional collecting.

Hobby - as a kind of occupation is called today, attracts a lot of people. Collecting minerals and stones is a hobby that does not require a certain time of day. Although some types of collectables depend on science, knowledge of any skills is not always required, as many items of the same type make for a rather amazing composition.

Collectors are the people on whom the value of a collection depends. There are many types of collectables, such as collecting coins, recipes, stones, minerals, and unique collections. Among them are stones and minerals, the unique sets that require special attention from the owner. Many people are interested in collecting different stones of different colors. The collection of stones is one of the most unusual collections. The colors and shapes of these stones are unique and unusual. Often this is done by those who are passionate about history and geology. Stones are collected both from the Earth's surface and from under it. Collecting stones and minerals is an activity that will allow you not to make large investments. But knowing about all types of stones and minerals, a good collector can gain a lot of value from this collection because each found stone or mineral has its origin history. There are many types of stones. For example, the same type of stone can change geometric shapes over time and composition, as they are affected by the weather. And also, it is on this that the shape and color of the stone depend. They tell the whole truth about the past. Those separate stones, without touching foreign objects, are well stored. Geologists are especially interested in minerals. Knowing the history of the finds will allow us to determine the time of origin of both minerals and stones. For collectors, all minerals and stones are described, and the vessels where they are stored have inscriptions with names.

Collecting stones and minerals is an amazing and interesting hobby that attracts adults and cute children. But besides a hobby, collections can bring not a small and quite tangible income. Whatever type of collecting a person does is always interesting and profitable.

Collecting stones is considered one of the most unique and unusual activities most people enjoy. Many people think that collecting stones is more suitable for young children, as they are always interested in finding and collecting stones of different colors and sizes. It is always easily accessible and exciting. But not only children are engaged in collecting stones. People who are related to geology are fond of this type of activity.

Why is This Activity so Interesting?

Some had already asked this question when it turned out that one of their friends was fascinated by such a collection. Stone rocks carry a real mystery as they reveal to us the true history of the origin of the Earth. The Earth is composed of many different rocks. Already those that are found on the surface, there are hundreds of thousands of species, as well as inside the Earth. Scientists have established the main differences between rocks depending on their origin since the particles from which they are formed have a different combinations. All fragments of stones are unique in size and color, depending on the type of rock. They are constantly changing; rain and wind influence the formation of their composition and shape. And only through research can geologists recreate the history of the planet.

As mentioned earlier, people who consider themselves in the field of geology are engaged in collecting, but often they are not geologists;

this science studies minerals, ore, and rocks to contribute to science, but not for personal reasons. Rockhounding can be very exciting and amazing, as any hobby should be primarily for the soul.

Rockhounding Basics

Sometimes it happens that the collection starts itself. First, one pebble appears in the house - I liked it at the exhibition. The second - fit into the interior. And then the excitement comes; you learn to appreciate the beauty of nature and see pictures in minerals. But sometimes, the idea to create a collection appears before the actual stones, and with various confusions, it is unclear where to start.

There is a "shortcut" here: ready-made collections of minerals. You know, those trays (often plastic) in which the stones lie are under the already applied signatures. But, firstly, the meaning of such a collection is not entirely clear, it can neither be supplemented nor reduced, and each sample is unremarkable. Secondly, fakes are often sold in such sets.

So it is better to choose each stone personally, slowly, and thoughtfully. To get started, here are a few tips.

1. Any of the agates. Agate has wide varieties; later, you will want to study and get them all when the collection grows. But for starters - how without agate?
2. Jasper. The same story as with agate.
3. Monochrome stone. There are many options - amethyst, aventurine, and jade.
4. Black or white stone. Shungite, for example, or white quartz.
5. A stone with a unique color. For example, malachite, charoite or turquoise.
6. Stone with iridescence. A tiger's eye or a labrador will do here (although their play of light is completely different,

so instead of "or" it's better to use "and").

7. "Metal" stone - such as hematite or pyrite. These stones are remarkable not only for their weight but also for their ability to retain cold and heat for a long time.
8. Organic stone - at least to figure out what it is, and not to prove to everyone that organic stones do not exist. There are many examples - pearls, coral, amber, ammonite.
9. A stone of an unusual shape. A geode, a raw crystal, a shard - anything but different, allowing you to see minerals in their diversity.
10. A rare stone - when the foundation is already there. For example, ametrine or larimar.

History of Rock Collection

The Urals is a stone belt, a mountainous country stretching from the Kara Sea coast to Kazakhstan's steps, the border between Europe and Asia. The length of the Ural Mountains from north to south is more than 2000 km; the width is from 50 to 150 km. According to the assumptions of various geologists, the Ural Mountains formed about 400 million years ago.

In historical sources, the Ural Mountains were first mentioned at the end of the 11th century in The Tale of Bygone Years. The name "Ural Mountains" appeared in the 18th century - this is what the geographer and historian Vasily Tatishchev called them. Translated from the Tatar language, "Ural" means "stone belt". Before this, the mountains were called Hyperborean and Riphean. Translated from the Bashkir language, "үр *ör" height, elevation, as a result, the word was transformed into the current Ural. The fact that life in the Urals arose in ancient times is evidenced by petrified trees with pronounced woody longitudinal stripes and bark.

Fossils include imprints of plants that lived on Earth in bygone eras. However, only an insignificant part of extinct plants and animals turns into fossils. Luckily, the school museum has rocks that clearly show the imprints of ferns, leaves, and grasses.

The Southern Urals is the widest part of the Ural Mountains. The South Ural Mountains are the remains of the former mountain system, which covers not only the entire area of the modern Chelyabinsk region but also the main part of Bashkortostan and the territories located to the east of our region. Scientists believe that the ancient ocean was located at this place. Fossils of molluscs that lived in our seas, lakes and rivers - traces of ancient creatures' lives once again prove our lands' marine origin.

Walking along the river bank or along a country road, you probably found an unusually shaped stone that looks like a petrified finger - unique minerals that look like arrowheads. These are belemnites or belemnites - a detachment of extinct cephalopods from a subclass of two-gills. Predators were probably good swimmers; they had fins, large eyes, horny jaws and an ink bag. The tentacles had hooks. Belemnites are related to modern octopuses, cuttlefish and squid. The unique form of belemnite - "devil's finger" - gave rise to many myths about its origin.

From the disintegrated shells of coccolithophorids, calcareous silt arose, in abundance inhabited by worm-eaters. They passed all the silt through themselves, "ploughed" it entirely, leaving not a single particle in place, continuing the physical and chemical destruction of the limestone shells. It is unsurprising that the silt eaters completely mixed the sediment and destroyed the layering. This means that limestone, gypsum, and chalk are organogenic rocks, almost completely composed of ultramicroscopic shells of organisms living in the seawater's surface layer.

The Urals is a storehouse of building material and fuel. The brown coals of the Chelyabinsk basin extend from north to south for 170 km. The reserves are over 700 million tons. Rich deposits of peat have accumulated in the swamps of the region. More than 60 deposits of building stone (more than 1 billion cubic meters) and more than 20 deposits of building sands (about 150 billion cubic meters) have been explored.

The advantage of the Urals is that the mountain range is a real treasure trove of minerals. Believe only, but 48 types of minerals out of 55 mined are represented here. The mountains of the Urals are rich in deposits of coal, oil, and gas. In terms of reserves of platinum, asbestos, precious stones, and potassium salts, the Urals is one of the first places in the world.

The depths of the Ural Mountains contain more than two hundred different minerals. Such minerals valuable as rare-earth crystal and piezo quartz are mined in the region.

A special group of minerals in the Urals are precious and coloured stones. Bright green emeralds, pale lilac amethysts, sparkling diamonds, golden topazes and changeable red-green alexandrites have long been the pride of the Urals. Valuable artistic stones are also famous - colourful jasper, marbles, green malachite, pink eagle, and greenish-blue amazonite.

Precious and ornamental stones are found in three places - in the Ilmensky, Cherry mountains and near Plast - hyacinth, amethyst, opal, topaz, garnet, malachite, corundum, jasper, sapphire, ruby, sun, moon and Arabic stone, etc. The Ilmensky mountains are a real mineralogical museum. It is there that our schoolchildren while relaxing in country camps and sanatoriums, get acquainted with precious and ornamental stones. It is from the Ilmensky Reserve Museum that collections of coloured stones are brought.

Stone-cutting art received especially intensive development in the 18th-19th century. By 1726, self-taught stone cutters were already working here. By the beginning of the 21st century, artisans have gained access to the free mineral market. They are actively mastering advanced stone processing technologies, preserving the best traditions of this noble craftsmanship. The hands of the Ural craftsmen made wonderful stone products that adorn the best museums in the country.

The original art of our days - pictures of multi-colored stone chips. They are made with virtually no underdrawings. For creativity, artists use minerals such as chrome diapsid, charoite, carnelian, jade, malachite, serpentine, fluorite, jasper, vermiculite, muscovite, phlogopite, biotite, marble, quartz, amazonite, etc.

Many writers like to identify the Ural Mountains with a piggy bank or even a repository of all earthly riches and valuables, which may be hidden somewhere in the depths, under a complex system of underground passages guarded by vigilant guards, and which, alas, is not destined to be reached by a simple person.

It is impossible to live in the Urals and not know the tales of Pavel Petrovich Bazhov. He probably could be called the first writer who opened the Urals to the world in all its beauty, history, people, wealth of mountains, folk tales and legends, and its richest language. The main heroine of Bazhov's tales, The Mistress of the Copper Mountain - the keeper of mountain gems - appeared in the Bazhov park in the city of Zlatoust thanks to the mayor of the city and patrons. It took 500 tons of natural stone from 8 quarries to build the park.

Even more, the stone was needed by the Satka entrepreneur, who created an amazing medieval recreation area, "Sonka's Lagoon" - Ural Disney Land. In the circle classes, we "go" on a journey to these places. Some of the schoolchildren visited amazing places in Satka, where you can relax in winter and summer.

In addition to the variety of stone rocks of the Urals, extraterrestrial - "aliens" appeared. A stone meteorite-chondrite with a total weight of 200 kg (about 20 fragments) fell on June 11, 1949, on the territory of the Kunashak region. Undoubtedly, among the stones on the shores of our lakes, among large and small pebbles at the bottom, there are fragments of this celestial body that fell into these waters and took root in the silty shores of our reservoirs, primarily Lake Chebakul. According to the Chelyabinsk local historian Alexander Moiseev, one cobblestone from Kunashak was presented to the Vietnamese leader Ho Chi Minh when he visited the Urals. And in Kunashak, all sorts of space lovers are still digging the ground in search of meteorite fragments. Unfortunately, these specimens are not yet in the museum. We would also like to find fragments of the recent February meteorite

Who knows, maybe someone will be lucky. In the meantime, our museum does not have such finds, but there is a field of activity, passion, and interest.

Visiting the amazing places of the Chelyabinsk region in contact with the world of artisans. Travelling in the Urals is the way to the knowledge of rocks and minerals. Curious finds from different centuries open the door to the past: magnesium rocks (pumice), stored in the school museum, alloys of unknown origin, and fossils. One has only to take a closer look at how amazingly unique the rocks surrounding us are.

The main three types of rocks: are igneous, metamorphic and sedimentary.

Igneous rocks are products of the cooling and solidification of magma. This cooling can occur within the Earth's crust, giving rise to plutonic or intrusive igneous rocks such as granite, gabbro, etc.; or, when coming into contact with the atmosphere or the ocean, which originates volcanic or extrusive igneous rocks such as basalt, rhyolite or obsidian.

Metamorphic rocks are created through exposure, as igneous or sedimentary rocks are subjected over and over long periods to heat, moisture, and pressure. This is how granite is "transformed" into gneiss, limestone into marble, and shale into slate. It is unusual to find metamorphic rocks in geologically young territories such as Costa Rica, while they are common and abundant rocks in Cordilleras such as the Andes.

Sedimentary rocks are formed as a result of the action of atmospheric agents on pre-existing rocks. That is to say, the weathering is caused by the physical, chemical and biological agents to which the rock is exposed, which causes its fragmentation, and the products or sediments generated from the rock are transported to other places by the wind and rivers, among others, where they are gradually deposited in layers. The rocks resulting from this process are sedimentary rocks, which can be of the clastic type such as sandstone, shale and conglomerate, and chemical or evaporitic such as limestone and halite.

The Oldest Rocks

Canadian scientists have discovered what could be the oldest rocks on Earth in eastern Canada's Hudson Bay, dated to between 3.8 billion and 4.28 billion years old. Geologists found the samples from Montreal's McGill University in the Nuvvuagittuq green rock belt in the northern Quebec province. After measuring the isotopes of neodymium and samarium - two rare elements - in the rocks, they determined that their age dates back to between 3,800 million and 4,280 million years.

The oldest are rocks classified as "false amphibolites", which in the opinion of the researchers, are ancient volcanic deposits. Scientists believe that the Earth is almost 4.6 billion years old, so if their age is confirmed, these rocks will date to the early evolution of the Earth and the solar system when the planet was cooling enough to form a crust.

It is estimated that the Earth was formed 4,567 million years ago, so the Nuvvuagittuq rocks would be the first indication of the first crust. If the Earth is a little over 4,500 million years old, specifically about 4,567, and these are believed to be 4,280, they were formed about 300 million years after the formation of the Earth; this is practically the beginning of the history of the planet.

Until now, the oldest traces of the crust that had been found consisted of scattered mineral grains, called zircons, found in Western Australia. However, the oldest known rock was the Acasta Gneiss, found in northern Canada, in the Northwest Territories, with 4,030 million years old, almost 300 million years younger than the new Canadians.

Rocks from 3.8 billion years ago that came from the bottom of the oceans had also been found in Greenland, according to what the same magazine published in March 2007. All these findings will help analyze how and when the planet's tectonic phenomena were formed in its origins.

In their conclusions, the scientists recall that the remains of the most primitive Earth's crust are very scarce because they have been crushed and recycled inside the Earth due to plate movements.

The new Canadian rocks are important to geologists because of their age and chemical composition. They resemble other volcanic rocks in geological environments where tectonic plates collide. "This gives us unprecedented insight into the processes by which the Earth's crust was formed," said Carlson.

Remnants of the Earth's early crust are extremely rare because most of it has been crushed and recycled multiple times by plate tectonics.

The oldest rock formations in the Iberian Peninsula are in Cabo Ortegal (Galicia), with 1,160 million years and some barnacles with the taste of a clean sea. Only in Newfoundland, Poland and Australia, There are only three other places on the entire planet (Newfoundland, Poland and Australia) with rocks that old. Some theories defend that these four points were united when there was only one continent on Earth, Pangea, which fractured into the current five.

Ancient Use of Rocks

In the history of humanity, the stone was one of the first materials to be used to transform it into objects. The geographical region of Mesoamerica, an area currently occupied by Mexico, was no exception; many cultures flourished there and with them, a large production of utilitarian, decorative and spiritual elements made with this material.

The reason for using this material since primitive times is that it is a material that is easily obtained in nature and that it can be transformed by striking and primitive carving. Other materials were used during the lithic age: bone, wood, thatch and clay, for example. However, the stone is an element with exceptional resistance, which undoubtedly contributed to a greater number of relics.

In that region, it was widely used; today, it is enough to explore any of the anthropology museums or an archaeological zone to find a great diversity of these objects.

The varieties of stone used during this period responded mainly to the geographical availability of the different cultures. Basalt, limestone and tezontle were commonly used for buildings and everyday objects. Jade, obsidian, and onyx were used for ornamental objects and some tools.

The limestone was the main protagonist for ceremonial buildings so frequent in that period. A soft stone that is easy to extract, considering that the tools were rudimentary at that time. Once placed in its place inside the building, it was combined with mortar (a mixture made from crushed limestone), an equivalent to today's cement. Some of its uses were constructing bases, pillars, lintels and, in some cases, complete megalithic constructions.

Also noteworthy is the use of obsidian, an element categorized as volcanic or mineraloid glass. It was the most efficient natural material for cutting instruments and spear points and making decorative and spiritual objects. Black in color, with small variations in tone, has the peculiarity that when cut parallel to it, its color is black, but perpendicularly it is grey.

When talking about jade, subcategories of semiprecious stones are covered. In Mesoamerican cultures, jadeite in shades of blue to green was primarily used. Valued for its rarity, brightness and smoothness, perhaps none was as deeply rooted in the cultures of Mesoamerica as this one, with abundance, life and the cosmos being its most significant values.

Onyx, considered a semiprecious stone, was also used to make vessels, spear points, masks, and ornamental details. It is mostly black and white, but its hue can vary from orange, red, yellow, brown, reddish, white and brown, among others.

The types of stones mentioned are still obtained using modern extraction techniques. Limestone is one of the components of grey cement; it is also used as an ornamental stone in construction. Jade and obsidian have the details of their main use in the jewellery sector and the manufacture of ornamental objects. As for onyx, Mexico is currently one of the world's leading producers. In addition to their natural beauty, these materials have the historical burden of being used by ancient cultures.

Rocks: Used from Ancient Times to The Present Day

The various stones, minerals and other minerals are created by nature. The extraction of coal, granite, basalt, peat, salt, clay, and sand has been carried out by man since immemorial. At first, they mined them by hand, and today these works are carried out with the latest machines.

How Rocks Were Formed

For millennia, minerals accumulated in the surrounding world caked and formed layers in the Earth's crust. People gradually learned to use coal to heat their homes, extract salt for food, and stones for building houses facing buildings.

Rocks can be light and heavy, hard and soft, and strong and slightly porous. The durability of the material and its flexibility during processing depend on these indicators. The lightweight and porous stones weigh less. Such material is easier to process, but at the same time, it is less strong. When water enters the pores and freezes, cracks form in the material. As a result, a seemingly strong stone can crack over time.

Huge boulders and high mountains seem powerful and eternal. You look at them and think that nothing can destroy them - neither time nor natural elements. However, everything changes over time, including rocks. They are affected by water, precipitation, wind, sun, heat and frost. And although the destruction is very slow, it cannot be stopped. The shape and properties of minerals gradually change. Their changes are also associated with human activities. Man can destroy anything with the help of powerful technology. Man destroys mineral deposits faster than nature.

The Cycle of Rocks in Nature

The formation of any minerals begins with the release of fiery lava from the bowels of the Earth. She cools down and hardens. This is how igneous rocks are obtained (from the word magma - this is lava). Wind, moisture, and high and low temperatures crush stones.

Rocks move, settle and form deposits in a certain place. This is how sedimentary minerals are obtained. Over time, mountain ranges sink into the Earth's crust, where they melt and turn into lava. Lava again breaks out to the surface of the Earth, solidifies, and the birth of stones begins anew.

The Study

To study a stone, it must be sawn. And if not entirely, then at least partially, make a small cut. So you can find out its history, features and time of appearance. A detailed examination is carried out using a microscope.

The Most Common Rocks

Humanity uses different rocks in different ways - some more, some less. Among the most used:

1. Sand and clay are essential building materials. Without them, it is impossible to build structures and build roads. Dishes, bricks and even medicinal ointments are made from clay, and glass and concrete mixes are made from sand.
2. Coal is used as a fuel in its pure form and as a component of liquid fuel for combustion in boilers of power plants. This fossil fuel is also used in the chemical industry.
3. Granite has different shades; it is perfectly polished. They decorate the walls of buildings, the surface of dams and other structures.
4. Sandstones are green, yellow, grey, red and brown. For the design of facades of buildings, red and green are most often used.
5. Marble is easy to process. When grinding, the brightness of the pattern is slightly lost, and when polished, on the contrary, the distinctness of the veins

on the stone increases. The marble is colored grey and white. It is used in construction for the manufacture of mosaics and countertops.

6. Shales can be red-brown, dark grey, or black. This is a durable material; it can split into even thin plates. It is used for facing buildings outside and inside.

The Mining of Precious Minerals

In late February, scientists at Stanford University found a way to produce diamonds from hydrogen and carbon molecules in crude oil. However, for many centuries, humankind had to act the old-fashioned way - we tell how precious stones were mined before and how they are mined now.

Man began to use stones as tools about 2.6 million years ago: at first, they were primitive, practically unprocessed pieces of rocks that served as the simplest household tools. Later, our ancestors learned to make more advanced tools and weapons out of them, but for many millennia, the stones had an exclusively useful purpose.

However, with the development of civilization, some breeds began to be endowed with a sacred and aesthetic function, and, as a result, they acquired a completely different material value.

In ancient times, it was more likely not about mining but an accidental discovery of precious stones: bright pebbles that stood out against the background, for example, grey river pebbles, inevitably attracted people's attention. They were picked up in streams and on slopes when the rock accidentally came to the surface, gradually released under the influence of erosion and descending along with water flows. Such stones were used as jewellery, amulets, attributes of power or for ritual purposes. Later, when it became clear where the beautiful gems come from, they began to be mined purposefully, using the simplest shovels and picks from stones, durable sticks and deer antlers.

Such excavations were superficial since the tools were primitive. However, at that time, it already became obvious: if several gems were found in a small area in the neighbourhood, this area would be potentially rich in other valuable finds. In addition to collecting precious stones directly from the surface, they were also searched for in rock crevices. The crystals that had grown on the rock were chipped off with the help of more advanced tools - chisels, picks or crowbars.

But gems became truly valuable relatively recently: emeralds in India were known for 2 thousand BC, and diamonds - 1000-500 BC. Interestingly, the Hindus divided diamonds, like people, into four varnas: the most expensive - brahmins - white transparent crystals, then came rocks with a reddish tint - Kshatriyas, followed by greenish or yellowish vaishyas and the least valuable, grey and muddy.

In the Sinai Peninsula, turquoise began to be mined approximately 3400 BC, and in the burial places of Ancient Egypt, archaeologists found crafts using lapis lazuli, amazonite, garnet, emerald, and amethyst. For example, in the tomb of Tutankhamen, many pieces of jewellery trimmed with turquoise and lapis lazuli were found, and the legendary scarab beetle on the chest pendant of the pharaoh was carved from green volcanic glass.

After humanity invented not only statehood but also the exploitation of other people's labour, enslaved people were everywhere engaged in the extraction of precious stones. So, near Mount Zabara, a deposit is known in Egypt, which, according to written monuments, was already developed in 1650 BC. Another deposit near Aswan, a few dozen kilometres from the Red Sea coast, was developed under Pharaoh Sesostris III about 37 centuries ago. Mining enslaved people dug mines up to two hundred meters deep - up to 400 people could be here simultaneously. At the same time, all work was carried out in complete darkness since it was believed that the emerald was afraid of the light.

After the rock was split into pieces and always smeared with olive oil to distinguish between precious crystals, these mines of Aswan later became known as the cauldrons, or mines of Cleopatra, since the last queen of Hellenistic Egypt had a soft spot for emeralds and considered them the only stones truly worthy of her beauty and grandeur. The ancient Roman emperor Claudius Nero was also in awe of emeralds. He had a large stone of rich green colour, cut in the shape of a lens. Nero used it as a monocle when he watched the battles of gladiators in the arena. However, in the 20th century, French scientists established that it was not an emerald but perfectly clean and polished chrysolite.

Serendipity in Ceylon

Sri Lanka was one of the oldest, richest, and most famous gemstone mining regions, which retains this status today. Here, sapphire, ruby, garnet, alexandrite, amethyst, greenish-yellow cat's eye, magic moonstones, topaz, and tourmaline - more than 80 species in total became known here 600 years before our era. It is curious that one of the former names of the island, Serendip, is in some way associated with this fishery. So it was called by the Persians and other peoples similarly: the Romans - Serendivi, the Arabs - Serendib.

From this form comes the term "serendipity", denoting intuitive insight, the ability, drawing deep conclusions from random observations, to find something that was not sought intentionally.

Book 2
Rockhounding for Beginners

The collection of rocks in the wild can be a daunting task. You need to identify the right rocks for your project, carry them far enough from the source so that you can collect them without disturbing the site further, and then transport them back to your location. This requires a lot of planning and anticipation, and it's often a lot of work. However, you can reduce this work and make rock collection easier if you have the right tools.

Equipment & Tools

This chapter will explore the main equipment and tools you want to carry during your rockhounding adventures. Before you decide to buy, it's important to consider your budget, what you expect to take home, and how much you want to spend. If you need assistance deciding what tools you want, keep reading.

You'll learn to have the right equipment to get the most out of your rockhounding experience and expand your knowledge. You'll also learn how to identify, harvest, and find the best specimens for your collection.

This chapter will explore the main equipment and tools you want on hand during your rockhounding adventures, from recommended safety gear such as eye protection and gloves to collecting tools such as pry bars and brushes.

You'll also discover valuable resources such as eld guides, ultraviolet lights, and record-keeping aids that will help you navigate to a site, identify specimens, and keep track of your finds. Some critical tools include a good geology book, GPS, and an appropriate smartphone. Others are optional, such as a field journal, rock hammer, side-scan sonar, and a compass. The list is nearly endless. With a little research, you'll find little difference in the equipment you can use for rockhounding, depending on where you live.

"Safety first" is an important mantra on the trail, and practicing good practices early in your journey can prevent unpleasant surprises further down the line.

The "Eld Guide" series is especially useful for the unprepared and those who want to learn the basics of rock identification. Eld guides show you how to identify the most common minerals on the surface and in the subsurface and recognize and interpret petrographic and microstructural features.

Or bring along a notebook to write down your discoveries as they occur. Either way, the more prepared you are, the more successful you will be.

All the good rockhounds know that a good hat can mean the difference between a great adventure and a not-so-great adventure. A good hat should complement the style you're going for and can easily be switched with something else in case of a change of style, season, or weather. Every rockhound needs a good hat; it's the rockhound's job to keep their head safe, and a good hat can do that better than most.

The attire should be comfortable and versatile. Lightweight, long-sleeved shirts and pants are recommended. If the rockhounds were going to be doing long-distance jogging, hiking, etc., they might want to consider wearing joggers, shorts, or athletic shorts.

"Hiking boots should hug the ground to avoid blisters. Gaiters can make you trip or exacerbate a fall, so choose carefully. If you have trouble finding less technical models, look for the ones with breathable mesh uppers and avoid neoprene booties.

Optimal unaltered attire for rockhounding should be comfortable, appropriate, and modest. It should also be clean, preferably simply washed. The optimal attire is also comfortable while working to entice the next adventure. It should be comfortable while digging, and it should be considered fashion.

"Dressing your best" is not simply about what people wear. It's also about how they move - how they stand, what they sit on, how they walk and how they interact with their environment. When people successfully navigate their environment, they move in a way that is comfortable to them, which aligns with their style and helps them to interact with their environment in the way they want. Achieving this requires skills in three areas: how to listen, how to imitate, and how to modify our actions to adapt to situations in which we don't have.

When rockhounding, it is important to take precautions for your eyes. There are many different types of eye protection for rockhounding that you should consider before heading out.

The first type of eye protection for rockhounding is sunglasses. Sunglasses can protect your eyes from the sun's harmful UV rays and are also useful if you look at colorful rocks in the sky or on the ground. The second type of eye protection for rockhounding is safety goggles, which provide more protection than sunglasses. Safety goggles will safeguard your eyes from dust and debris while you are digging through rocks or sifting through

Various items can be used in rockhounding, such as gloves, safety goggles, and hammers.

Gloves are mostly used to protect the hands from sharp objects and rough textures. They are also helpful in protecting the hands from getting dirty or greasy while handling rocks.

Safety goggles help protect eyes from dust and debris that can get kicked up during rockhounding. They also prevent rocks from getting into the eyes when they are picked up or handled.

Hammers are used to breaking apart rocks to see what is inside them or to break them into smaller pieces so they can be picked up more easily.

When exploring, it is important to have a first aid kit with you.

Some things that should be in your first aid kit include:

- Bandaids
- Antiseptic ointment
- Gauze pads
- Alcohol wipes
- Tweezers

In addition to these tools, you will also need a good way to keep track of your finds. A simple daybook and pencil will do the trick, or you can use a more sophisticated rockhounding software program. Whichever way you keep track of your finds, ensure you are consistent so you can easily reference your records later. As a rockhound, you will need a few essential tools to help you in your journey. A good quality rock hammer is a must, a chisel, and a set of small picks. You will also need a strong magnifying glass to help you examine your findings. A good book on rocks and minerals is also essential for helping you identify what you find.

Many different tools and equipment are used for navigation and record-keeping when rockhounding. It is important to have the proper tools and equipment to find your way back to where you found the rock and keep track of the rocks you found.

Some of the navigation tools that are used for rockhounding include GPS devices, compasses, and maps. GPS devices can be very useful in finding your way back to a spot, and compasses can be used to help you find your way around in general. Maps can also be very helpful for navigation and keeping track of where you have been and what rocks you have found.

Various record-keeping tools can be used for rockhounding. These include notebooks, cameras, and labeling.

Joining a Rockhounding Club

Joining a rockhounding club is a great way to get started in the hobby of rockhounding. It is an amazing way to meet other people who share your interest in rocks and minerals and a great way to learn more about the hobby. There are a lot of different rockhounding clubs out there, so you should take some time to find one that's right for you.

Rockhounding is a great hobby for people of all ages. It's a great way to get outdoors and explore nature, and it's also a great way to find some amazing treasures. If you're considering joining a rockhounding club, here's what you can expect.

Most rockhounding clubs have a yearly membership fee, giving you access to all of the club's activities and resources. This includes access to the club's claims (areas where you're allowed to hunt for rocks), access to the club's equipment, and more. You'll also get access to the club's newsletter, which is a great way to stay up-to-date on all the latest rockhounding news.

In addition to the yearly membership fee, most clubs also have a small fee for each event or activity, and joining a rockhounding club is a great way to get started.

There are a lot of different rockhounding clubs out there, so you should take some time to find one that's right for you.

Once you've joined a club, you'll be able to participate in club activities like field trips, mineral shows, and more. You can also make use of the club's resources, like its library of rockhounding books and its network of experienced rockhounds. So if you're ready to take your rockhounding to the next level, joining a club is the way to go.

Laws and Regulations in Rockhounding

Each state has different laws, regulations, and rules regarding rockhounding. It would be beneficial if you had a permit to collect certain rocks and minerals in some states. In other states, there may be restrictions on where you can collect. It's important to research the laws in your area before you start collecting.

In addition to state laws, there may also be federal laws that apply to rockhounding. For example, if you plan to collect on federal lands, you must obtain a permit from the appropriate agency.

In the United States, rockhounding is regulated by the Federal Land Policy and Management Act of 1976. This law controls how rocks, minerals, and fossils can be collected on public lands. It is vital to follow these regulations to avoid potential fines or jail time.

Some regulations vary from state to state. For example, it is illegal in California to collect rocks in national parks without a permit. It would be helpful if you had a permit to collect fossils in New York on state-owned land.

Before you start rockhounding, ensure you are familiar with the laws and regulations in your region.

Where to Look

Rocks and minerals can be found everywhere, but finding beautiful ones requires knowledge, observation, and practice.

Let's discuss how different people look at rocks and minerals and what they mean to them:

An ordinary adult, as a rule, does not pay attention to them at all; he goes about his business stones. They don't exist for him until someone gets under his leg or is needed to drive the dog away.

The average child notices the stones and marvels at their shape and color. Children, as a rule, collect them indiscriminately or select them only according to some criteria they only understand.

The geologist, with his professional eye, notices every pebble. Still, he is interested in and accordingly gets into the backpack, only those that can contribute to completing a particular task at the moment. The designer, sculptor, and architect have their view of the stones.

The average stone collector seeks out specific types of stones as a hobby.

Real Rockhounds, extract samples of interest to them wherever possible and impossible. They make their way into mines, quarries, and other extraction places and dig in the dumps of old and existing mine workings. They conduct excavations in places little known to the rest of humanity; in the end, they exchange or even buy treasured stones from each other, gradually turning their home partly into an exposition of a geological museum, partly into impassable warehouses of boxes, boxes, bags of stones.

Okay, let's not go to extremes. Let us assume that we are no longer an indifferent category that does not notice anything. Noted at the beginning and not omniscient and ubiquitous rockhounds nutcases. Where can an ordinary interested person find beautiful stones for his modest collection?

And for free and for the benefit of the mind and health? To begin with, consider where the stones, beautiful and ordinary, come from. From the sky? Yes, it happens, but very rarely. In addition, they are unprepossessing in appearance.

Where and How Did Minerals Appear

Most of the stones were formed, so to speak, "under the ground," at great depths, at high temperatures, etc., pressures. Remember, we studied at school that the earth consists of a core, a soft mantle, and a crust? And to give to us. An idea of the relative thicknesses of these layers, was the earth compared to an apple?

The peel of an apple is the bark. The flesh of the apple is the mantle. Duck, in this "peel," stones were formed at different times - from millions to billions of years ago. The thickness of the "peel" is 30-40 km. By human standards, the depth is decent. And we call it "the firmament of the earth," but in a more global sense, it is a shaky contraption.

Nothing compared to the bottomless ocean of the mantle she floats on. And the earth's crust, now and then in one place, in another, "flattens" and warps. Some areas are moving towards others. Folds (mountains) appear, and the bark bursts at the seams (along the old and newly formed ones).

Molten masses rise from the mantle along fractures in the crust, sometimes reaching the surface and pouring out in the form of rapidly cooling lava. And sometimes getting stuck in the depths of the earth's crust and hardening, cooling, crystallizing there for millennia.

At the same time, the most diverse ones occur in different parts of the cooling body or outside it. Combinations of chemical and physical processes. And somewhere, with a unique combination of some factors and certain circumstances. Rock crystal is formed, somewhere rubies, somewhere other minerals. Years passed, more precisely millennia and "million years," the earth's crust continued to warp and break. Some of its sections rose; others sank into the depths. The rising areas were destroyed by surface forces (wind, water, sun, etc.) and some areas of our petrified body. Appeared on the surface in the form of rocks, for example. And along with them, some deposits of gems or. Came to the surface or became closer to it and more accessible to man.

Further destruction of the rocks led to the "pulling" of stones along the earth's surface. Large blocks could move simply by rolling down the slope as they were crushed. Carried by streams and rivers. Well, that's enough about the genesis (about the origin). All this was necessary only to ensure that logically. Figure out where to look for pebbles.

So, where are we looking for:

- Rocks, rock outcrops, collapses near rock outcrops. Here, artificial outcrops of rocks such as tunnels, cuts of roads and railways into rocks, quarries, etc., must be taken into account.
- Banks of rivers, streams, lakes, seas, and oceans. Sometimes, according to the fragments of gems found on the bank of the stream, you can go to the root exits and the vein where these fragments come from. Remember Jack London's famous story? There, the truth was about gold, but the principle is the same. Sometimes, a beautiful pattern of jasper or Agate can be hidden inside a nondescript pebble found on the shore. Chalcedony. Or the pebble might be a geode filled with amethyst or rock crystal.

Where to Search and Find Precious Stones?

Do you want to learn where to look for gemstones? Remember that the world's most valuable gemstones and minerals appear in specific and highly restricted places. For this cause, we have created a brief guide that provides tips so that you can find gemstones near where you live.

Remember that the different types of precious stones are formed due to very complex geological processes such as the differentiated crystallization of certain types of magmas, solidification of hydrothermal fluids enriched in certain chemical elements, the metamorphism of rocks and minerals, and the hydrothermal alteration of rocks that make up the crust.

Also, it is important to know that precious stones can be found in primary and secondary deposits, so you must learn the basics of these topics to have a better chance of finding a high-value mineral. We also leave you some tips so you can search and find precious stones in your country.

- Analyze a geological map: One of the best ways to find precious stones is to analyze the geological maps of your country, province, or city. Geologists have worked mapping the rocks and minerals of your country for decades and have identified prospective areas for the formation of precious stones; identify those areas and start there.

- Learn about mineral deposits: Precious stones are formed in very restricted and special geological environments; If you learn the basics about prospective mineral deposits for gemstone formation, you will have a better chance of finding those valuable minerals and stones.

- Learn to distinguish precious stones: One of the main mistakes people have is confusing common minerals of low value with precious stones. For this reason, we recommend you learn to identify the main gemstones or minerals you want to find.

- Study what type of gemstones can be found near where you live: Keep in mind that gemstones will not exist in all places; each country or region will have certain types of gemstones that other countries will not have. Investigate what minerals and stones exist in your country so that you can go in search of them and not spend time looking for precious stones that may not exist where you live.

- Research Old and Working Gemstone Mines in Your Country: One of the best ways to search for and find gemstones in your country is to do so around old and working mines. Investigate the location of those mines and start your search there, always respecting private property since you will not want to have problems with the companies that own those mines.

- Buy the right tools to search for gemstones: Don't forget to buy the right tools to search for gemstones and analyze their physical properties. The basic tools are a geologist's hammer, a 10 and 20x magnifying glass, hardness pencils, a magnet, acid, GPS, geological and topographical maps, appropriate clothing for the area's climate, a camping tent, a compass, and a backpack.

- Maintain a good physical condition: To search and find precious stones, you will surely have to walk a lot and through places sometimes of medium to difficult complexity. Therefore, we recommend you work on your physical condition before you venture out searching for precious gems.

- Ask for advice on how to look for precious stones from geologists in your country: Geologists are the right people who know everything about minerals and precious stones that exist in your country, they have studied for many years about the most suitable deposits of precious stones in your area, it is recommended that you ask them for advice so that your search is successful.

Dangerous Minerals to look out for

Today I came across a list of the ten most toxic and potentially deadly minerals that crystallize in rocks and represent a dangerously deceptive stone beauty. These stones can cause serious harm to health, even just being beautifully placed on a shelf as an interior decoration or a sample from a collection.

We are so used to seeing all kinds of minerals in our daily lives that we do not stop thinking about the secrets they all keep in their curious shapes and colors. A mineral is considered a natural, inorganic, homogeneous substance with a defined chemical composition, and although we tend to contemplate them with fascination, some of them can be deadly.

Today we are going to show you which are the eleven most dangerous minerals among the most dangerous. Professor Gordon Brown made the selection of the Stanford University of Earth, Energy, and Environmental Sciences. Not only do minerals with exotic names appear in them, but also many others that we are more accustomed to, such as Pyrite or Quartz.

11. Cinnabar or Mercuric Sulfide

Cinnabar is the main source of mercury as it is its natural form. It occurs in granular and crystal form in areas close to volcanic activity and hot springs and has been mined since Neolithic times. It is insoluble, and when oxidized, it produces toxic compounds such as methyl mercury and dimethyl mercury. It is fatal in small concentrations and can be absorbed through the respiratory tract, intestines, or skin.

These two compounds produced by Cinnabar can seriously affect the nervous system and create problems in the development of fetuses and children. Even so, its intense vermilion red color led to magical and medicinal qualities being attributed to it both in the East and in Pre-Columbian America, being used by the Chinese as an ornament and medicine to restore vitality and by some tribes in northern Peru in their ceremonial masks.

10. Galena

Galena is a lead sulfide mineral and the main way to obtain it. It comes in shiny silver-colored cubic forms, and although its main component is lead, it may contain small amounts of silver. Its beauty made it used in ancient Egypt to make cosmetic powders.

But what they didn't know about this relatively insoluble mineral is that it can cripple the developing nervous system of fetuses and children and cause cardiovascular disease in adults. It is not as toxic as lead, but it accumulates in our bodies until it reaches levels that can be dangerous.

9. Pyrite

Pyrite is also called "fool's gold" due to its close resemblance to gold, but it is an iron sulfide with 53.48% sulfur. It is a major contaminant of streams and groundwater due to its mining waste. Its oxidation releases toxic metals and metalloids highly poisonous to humans, such as arsenic.

This mineral is quite a disuse since, although it was used to extract sulfur and sulfuric acid in the past, these are currently obtained as by-products of natural gas or crude oil processing. This means that pyrite is practically only extracted for studies and scientific research.

8. Fluorite

Fluorite is composed mainly of fluorine and calcium, is relatively soluble, and has a striking purple color. It is mainly used in the foundry of iron and steel, cosmetics, and the optical industry to create certain glasses and microscopic and telescopic lenses.

Its excess in the body can cause severe bone disorders, resulting in an irreversible disease called skeletal fluorosis. Currently, its main producer is China, and it is no coincidence that millions of people affected by this disease have already been counted in the province of Guizhou.

7. Quartz

Quartz, also known as silicon dioxide, is one of the most abundant minerals in the earth's crust and can occur in different forms such as silica sands, glass, stones, and Tripoli. It is used by the oil industry or hydraulic fracturing to manufacture electronic and optical components.

But be careful because prolonged exposure to its fine particles can cause lung cancer, kidney disease, immune problems, and silicosis, which is the deposition of silica dust in the lungs, causing respiratory and heart failure.

6. Chrysotile or White Asbestos

Tied for number 6 with Quartz, Chrysotile is a magnesium hydroxy-silicate normally used as an ornamental rock. However, it was used to manufacture fabrics and insulation in the past. Although countries like Russia and China continue to be the largest exploiters of this mineral, its mining is also prohibited in more than 50 countries.

The fact that the mineral has been declared carcinogenic by the World Health Organization (WHO) has a lot to do with this ban. Inhalation of its solid particles can cause pneumoconiosis, which causes damage to lung tissue and ends up leading to cancer. Even so, countries like the United States still use it to produce different products such as clutch bands or disc brake pads.

5. Potassium Feldspar

Potassium feldspar or K-feldspar is a group of potassium aluminum silicate minerals that includes orthoclase, microcline, and adularia. They are currently used to manufacture porcelain, electrical insulators, ceramic enamel, glass, abrasive or even gems with some variants.

It consists of small amounts of radioactive uranium that form radon gas, which the EPA says is the prime cause of lung tumor in the United States. As if this were not enough, it is also a major source of lead emissions into the environment.

4. Phenakite

Phenakite is part of the neosilicate family and an important source of beryllium. This toxic element can induce lung cancer and other serious inflammatory lung diseases, such as chemical pneumonitis or berylliosis, which causes pulmonary fibrosis and granulomas in different body organs.

But beryllium is also used for many other things. Today it is used in X-ray tubes, as a neutron moderator in nuclear reactors or as a structural material in satellites, high-speed aircraft, spacecraft, missiles and elements for communication devices. . It was also used in the ceramic industry. Still, in that case, the multiple lung diseases it caused meant its use was restricted.

3. Erionite

Erionite is a naturally existing fibrous mineral belonging to the silicate mineral group called zeolites. It is usually found in volcanic ash altered by groundwater and weather and in some rock formations such as basalts or rhyolites. It is on the list of 118 things that cause cancer, according to the WHO, and its extraction was stopped in the late 1980s.

Exposure to this mineral can cause diseases such as mesothelioma, a form of cancer that develops in a protective lining that covers many of our internal organs called the mesothelium. Some of its symptoms are respiratory difficulties due to pleural effusion, chest pain, and unexplained weight loss.

2. Hydroxyapatite

Hydroxyapatite is a naturally existing mineral form of calcium apatite, and elements such as phosphorous in garden fertilizer or fluoride in tap water can come from this mineral. Apatite has several variants, Hydroxyapatite being one of the most important components of dental enamel, and its sister Fluorapatite is used in water to prevent cavities.

Healthy teeth and bones are important, but exposure to Hydroxyapatite during mining or processing is dangerous, as it can form deposits on heart valves and arteries. Many people die each year from this, as it can lead to restricted or even completely blocked blood flow.

1. Crocidolite or Blue Asbestos

Crocidolite, also called blue asbestos, is a fibrous variety of riebeckite and is considered the most dangerous mineral in the world. Its name means incorruptible in Greek, and its low thermal conductivity and high resistance to heat mean that, like other types of asbestos, it is used to manufacture insulation, heat-resistant materials, and roof coatings.

Also used as an ornamental stone known as tiger's or hawk's eye, exposure can cause fatal diseases such as lung tumor, Mesothelioma, or Asbestosis. This mineral caused at least 1,000 deaths among miners who extracted it and residents of Wittenoom, Australia, between 1943 and 1966.

How to Start and Organize your Rock Collection

Okay! If you have reached a point where you have a considerable number of pieces at home, say more than 25, it means that you are on your way to becoming a potential mineral collector (or not).

It must be clear that collecting is not the same as accumulating. If you have a lot of stones, however beautiful they may be, all packed together in a container, adorning your living room, forgive me for saying. That is not a collection; it is simply the beginning of the Diogenes syndrome.

A collection of minerals or anything else must follow an order and guidelines we should define from the beginning and not get out of them unless you want a lot of work and entertainment. It must also provide reliable information about the pieces through labels or cards.

Some examples of collections could be the following, and I think the difference is quite clear.

It is necessary to start from the base that the definitive collection does not exist; each collection is unique and a reflection of the collector who owns it, although in the case of minerals, the collections are usually quite standardized, and it is rare to find collectors who do not follow any which I am going to show you next.

Guidelines:

- Systematic collection: An international association is dedicated to controlling and managing the existing mineral species. They determine, among other things, whether a species is valid or not based on its characteristics, chemical composition, and other issues. The IMA (International Mineralogical Association). Carrying out a systematic collection consists of gathering as many species accepted by the IMA as possible (currently around 6000, and it is estimated that 30-50 new species are identified and accepted each year).

- Geographical collection: in this case, the collections are delimited to certain areas, countries, or regions. Many collectors only collect minerals from their country of origin, for example, and the aim is to collect all the minerals that appear in the chosen area.

- Aesthetic collection is the most striking since the main value sought in pieces is that they are beautiful to look at. Minerals are sought here where the perfection of the crystals, the color, the brightness, or the combination of all of them stand out. It is undoubtedly the type of collection that most attract people, both those who understand and those who do not, and the main factor by which a person begins to collect. The first stone always comes home because it seems beautiful to us.

- Thematic collection: some collectors focus solely on one type of mineral, collections exclusively of quartz, for example, or other species such as fluorites, also groups such as garnets, tourmalines and a little more specialized are the twin collections, fluorescent minerals the criteria to choose from here are endless.

Apart from this, some collectors choose to make a second sieve based on the size of the pieces:

- Museum size: the pieces exceed 18 cm. Private collections with pieces of this size are rare since space is usually one of the most limiting factors that collectors encounter in developing their hobby. Apart from this, it must be taken into account that the ease of finding good quality pieces of this size is very limited; Whether we collect the pieces ourselves (they are difficult to find, extract and get home intact) or if we buy them since the price of minerals increases exponentially depending on their size.

- Showcase collection: a distinction is usually made between a cabinet (from 10 to 18 cm) and a small cabinet (between 5 and 10 cm). They are one of the most attractive collections; the pieces have the ideal balance between the size and perfection of the samples, especially in the case of small cabinets.

- They are usually displayed in showcases, as their name suggests, and are ideal for showing off to visitors.

- Collection of micro amounts: The pieces are usually less than 1 cm, and usually, some instrument is needed, such as a thread counter, hand magnifying glass, or binocular microscope, to be able to observe their crystals. They have the advantage that they take up very little space, and the beauty and perfection that we can find in the crystals of our samples are incomparable.

Order:

You can order the collection according to the criteria you like the most, as long as it is consistent and continued over time.

- Numerical order: consists of assigning each mineral in our collection a number, usually correlative. It is the easiest way

- Alphabetical order: at first, it may seem like a good option, but I do not recommend its use unless you have a good database on your computer, since when you start to have a considerable number of pieces, moving the location of each one of them and their tokens to make room for the new one that enters can become a real madness, imagine having to move 1000 pieces and tokens from their position, one by one, every time you go to add a new mineral to your collection. It is impossible. The only option here is that they are automatically ordered in the database, and it tells you the place (drawer, box, showcase, and its position within it) where you store it and store the pieces according to their order entry in the collection, not its name.

- Scientific order: it is preferred by those who make systematic collections, and in it, the pieces are ordered according to one of the traditional classifications, such as the Strunz classification, or the DANA classification (I recommend that you expand the information with a biography if What I am naming sounds Chinese to you, you could take a look at the DANA Crystallography Manual, for example,)

- Geographical Order: its name says it all; we organize the collection according to the origin, so we can keep together all the minerals that come from the same mine or the same country naturally; it is usually used by collectors who follow a geographical criterion in its collections

- Personal order: the imagination rules, resulting in the most varied collections. We could order our minerals by colors, for example, or by their weight, their size; anything you can think of is valid, and you like it

Once we have decided how we are going to set up our collection, each mineral must have an associated card in a database, where we can record all the characteristics of the mineral that are of interest, the exact origin of the mineral being basic (mine, place, town, province, country), and to which other sections are usually added, such as the date and method of acquisition. Traditionally, copies of these cards or labels were made by hand: one as a summary, which always accompanied the piece in the same place where it was stored, and another, longer and with more data, which was kept in filing cabinets exclusively for this.

Nowadays, thanks to computers, this last type of card has been replaced by others of computer support; we have many specialized databases for mineral collecting, and if you are a bit handy, you can even program one to your liking and add as many fields as you want, including photos, without taking up physical space in your home.

On the other hand, the "summary" label must be kept, even if we no longer do it by hand but instead make a copy with the printer.

(the pieces are between 5 and 2.5 cm) and thumbnails (between 2.5 and 1 cm), and they receive this name because they are kept in small individual containers. It is common for most novice collectors to begin by making this type of collection, with samples that can be easily purchased at street markets, cheap, and presented in 4x4 cm cardboard boxes. Later, if the collector decides to continue acquiring pieces of this size, he usually chooses to store them in

Collectors have found various creative ways to display their rocks: under glass tabletops, wire wrapped in rain chains, sewn into wall hangings and secured to various supports, including mantel surrounds. Natural stones and carved rocks are used as game pieces worldwide.

What can I do with my rock collection?

You can do many things with your old rock and mineral collection, like sell it, donate it to college, high school, or museum, trade it, or even make some amazing decorations, jewelry, and games for your children's home or even for you.

How do you Present a Rock?

One of the convenient and most favorite ways to display rocks in a jar is by using a vintage-style mason fruit jar. The best part about using vintage-style mason jars is that you can find them with different colored glass, from clear to blue to even pink! The most common colors are light, of course, blue and green.

How do you Organize Rock Collections?

Identify, label, and catalog your collection. Decide how to classify your samples. Choose which samples to display. Organize and display your prized pieces. Properly save the rest of the collection.

How are Small Rocks and Crystals Displayed?

Rock and Mineral Exhibits

Its textures and tiny crystals should not be touched. Attractive rocks from the holidays or your garden display well in decorative baskets or bowls. If you have a lot of tiny rocks, place them in tall parfait jars.

How are Painted Rocks Displayed Outside?

Ways To Show Painted Rocks. Put them on a shelf. Add them to potted plants or garden containers. Keep them in bowls or vases. Try using a mini easel. Use a chocolate container to store them. Make use of a display container. Recycle a large frame for display.

How Is A Mineral Collection Displayed?

The best way to display minerals is in a well-lit glass front or visible cabinet where the beauty of the minerals is on display. Due to the high cost of breakfronts, many collectors keep their specimens in less expensive organized drawers.

How do you Display Crystals and Stones?
Mounted Glass
A simple spiked mount purchased from a hobby store or even eBay can display crystals and illuminate a shelf or window ledge. Display gemstones atop a stack of books, among houseplants, or beside photo frames and keepsakes. You can also arrange several together to create the look of an adult rock collection.

How are Garden Rocks Stored?
For example, plastic sheeting is best to prevent the rocks from sinking into the ground if the stones are placed on dirt or gravel. On the other hand, if they are going to be installed over an existing base, then landscape fabric with self-adhesive backs will do the trick!

How are Geodes Displayed?
Organize on a Shelf
"I love to display geodes on a shelf among books and other antique collections," says Fischel-Bock. Add your stones to any front shelf for a touch of earthy, natural decor. You can also incorporate stones into a bookcase set up by finding a pair of geode bookends. They are functional but decorative.

How are Loose Gemstones Displayed?
Let's start with security. Every store's circumstances are different, but placing loose stones in small trays of no more than three and spreading the trays throughout the cabinet is a good way to deter break-and-grab thieves and mitigate loss.

How are Painted Rocks Waterproofed?
Choose from spray-on or brush-on sealants. The choice is yours. Wait for the paint to dry completely. Apply multiple coats. Spray from

a distance or brush in even motions. Let it dry in the sun. Additional tips for preserving painted rocks.

Is it Illegal to Leave Painted Rocks?

While some people love finding fresh, painted rocks, not everyone loves them. Some people think of them as garbage and rubbish. In state and national parks, it is illegal to hide them, and they are considered trash.

What do Rockhounds do with their Rocks?

Their collections are carefully classified by name and type and labeled with the date and place they were found. Serious hounds frequent rock and mineral shows, trade specimens, and own cutting and polishing equipment. Casual collectors are a completely different breed of rock collectors.

Where can I Place my Crystals?

Place one anywhere near the front door of your house; many people will place one in a pot or on a door frame. Both obsidian and hematite are also used in this way as they are also known for their protective qualities. Um, yes, there are also crystals for the kitchen.

How to Decorate with Crystals?

Decoration ideas with crystals and stones to add a touch of glamor

Geode lights and lavender crystal decoration idea. White stones are hanging from a gold chandelier. Polished Stone Drawer Knobs. Reflection of raw amethyst frames. Gray marbled stone bookends. Low lamplight on the rocks. Blue Agate Framed in White.

How do you Polish River Rocks without a Glass?

You can polish smooth river rocks and pebbles with jojoba oil after washing them with soapy water. You will require to reapply after a few weeks as this is not a permanent result. Oil does not polish rocks; it just gives them a shiny appearance that refreshes them and makes them look dewy.

Can you Varnish Rocks?

Can painted rocks be sealed with varnish? With a brush over varnish, you only need a thin coat, so be careful during the application process, but a spray varnish usually has a flow control built into the spray system, so you only need to keep it 30cm away from rocks and spray for a few seconds.

How to Polish a Stone

Polishing is the final process in the processing of stone, as a result of which its surface acquires a mirror shine, and the rock's pattern, color, and structure are revealed. As a rule, the stone is polished with special devices and in several stages.

- Before polishing the stone, it is necessary to polish it to remove all traces after cutting the stone. Grinding can be divided into three operations: peeling (rough grinding), grinding, and finishing-burnishing. If you don't have a stone machine, sand the glass.

- To do this, take a glass (6-10 mm thick), pour abrasive powder on it, moisten it with water and grind in circular motions. You can also use fine sandpaper for sanding. If you grind a stone on a machine, use a cast iron, lead, or copper wheel. Make sure that the surface of these circles is even and smooth.

- To polish the machine, remove the faceplate, then the protective (plastic) housing, and wash them thoroughly with soap and a brush. Put the cleaned parts back in place, fix the polishing wheel, pour a pinch of powder on the wheel, moisten the powder with water and rub it in a circle. You can use aluminum, zinc, chromium oxide, and diamond dust as polishing powders. Turn on the motor and polish the stone. But to polish the stone on the machine, you can use felt or cloth.

- Make circles 10-20 mm thick from these materials and stick them on the cast-iron faceplate with shellac, sealing wax, or a mixture of sealing wax with rosin or tar, but lay sheet rubber between the metal and the polished material. Before polishing, slightly moisten felt, felt cloth circles. When grinding or polishing, bring the stone up and press gently; the movement of the hand should be directed against the wheel's rotation.

- If you need to polish hard stones such as granite, or jasper, use wheels made from alder, aspen, poplar, or beech wood. But make sure that they rotate at a speed of 200 revolutions per minute; at a low speed, the polishing is better. Stones of the same type have different polishing abilities. Selecting an individual amount and combination of powders, disk rotation speed, and pressure force is necessary for each stone.

- To check the quality of the polishing of the stone, wipe the polished surface with a clean cloth, stand near the switched-on electric lamp and try to find the Reflection of the hair of the burning lamp on the surface of the stone. If the Reflection is visible, then the polishing was successful.

- If you do not have polishing tools, then replace the polishing of the stone with varnishing using a colorless varnish.

How are Stones Processed?

Even though working with a stone is difficult and requires physical strength and professional tools, it can be done at home. The processing of stones always begins with a thorough cleaning of what has accumulated over many years on the surface of the stones. As a rule, to begin with, stone processing is done with water, brushes, scrapers, and various degrees of aggressiveness with detergents. This helps remove the initial coating of dirt, and to remove lime or calcite deposits from the stone, more serious compounds are used, such as hydrochloric or oxalic acid. Each stone is unique, as it is a work of nature, so any of them need to choose the right approach.

Processing should show all the natural beauty of the stone; sometimes, it has to be cut or polished for a long time. The decision to cut is especially difficult, as often the stones are completely covered, and it is impossible to guess from which angle the pattern inside will be more beneficial. These skills come only with experience, but you can learn to handle the stone carefully much earlier. How it is necessary to handle a stone is determined primarily by its hardness, toughness, brittleness, and heterogeneity of properties. The most heterogeneous mineral is mica, so it's processing in different directions is different. Stone processing at home can include cutting, turning, grinding, polishing, and carving stone. The stone is often cut with a thin diamond disk since the cutting tool's edge must be harder than the mineral.

It is also possible to cut stone with soft metals, provided an abrasive dissolved with water is supplied to the cut site. But diamond saws speed up the process and minimize the loss of sawn stone. Coolants are used to avoid cracking of the stone from high temperatures caused by friction. Kerosene is used on industrial hermetically sealed machines, but at home, it is flammable, and it is more convenient to take water with soda dissolved in it instead. If you have the opportunity and desire, you can assemble a small stone cutting machine at home, but you can also use diamond files, or a grinder saw. For safety reasons, wearing a protective mask and goggles when working and ventilating the room is necessary.

The stone to be processed is firmly clamped in a vise on a table or other surface convenient for the master. To avoid damaging the countertop, a substrate is needed from below, after which the vise is tightly tightened since a loosely fixed stone can damage the instrument. A water container should be within walking distance to wash off dirt when it appears and cools the stone. A preliminary furrow is made on the stone with a file, after which sawing begins along it. Sometimes one stone requires several cuts, and first, you must decide how to perform them at the lowest cost. The difficult thing is to cut the stone lengthwise, making flat cabochons. When little is left before the end of the work, it is necessary to exercise the greatest care to not break off the stone.

The file often jams on the last millimeters of work, especially during manual processing. To not break the stone with an awkward movement, carefully pull it out of the vise and release the file with the same careful movements. To avoid this situation, you can cut alternately from two sides to the middle, so there is less chance of chipping off the corner and breaking the unfinished work. Cleaning the cuts also requires a lot of time and effort; this work will require sandpaper of the coarsest fraction. The cut is processed with it until the deepest scratches and dents disappear. If necessary, the side and opposite sides of the processed stone are smoothed with the same paper. Working with sandpaper also requires constant wetting of the stone and is sometimes carried out directly in a water container.

After large scratches and bumps are smoothed out with coarse sandpaper, the stone is rubbed with a soft cloth and examined for smaller bumps and chips. Such roughness requires processing with a finer sandpaper, after which the stone is washed again, wiped with a soft cloth, and examined in good light to detect small defects. When using finer sandpaper up to zero, it is necessary to completely level the stone, leaving no scratches, roughness, dents, and bulges on it. Sandpaper of zero number polishes the stone, giving it a shine. Before final polishing, it is required to check the stone very carefully since GOI paste can get into cracks and scratches, spoiling the whole result. The final polishing is done with felt or felt.

It is faster and more convenient to polish using a machine with a rotating shaft, onto which a small quantity of GOI paste is squeezed out. The stone, for some time, turns concerning the machine in different directions, and polishing occurs relatively quickly. Manual work is done the same way, but much more time will be spent since it is not very convenient to polish the stone by hand. It is also possible to fix the stone motionlessly for polishing and work with a drill or screwdriver with the appropriate device. This stage of work is called polishing, or polishing, and it is necessary for the self-processing of stone. Polishing closes the existing micro-holes, in which the stone is destroyed faster.

Natural stone has been one of the best building materials for many years. Previously used as the main building material, it is now more used as a finishing material. Countertops, window sills, fireplaces, and floors are made from it, and they decorate the interior and exterior.

The influence of time leaves its traces even on such eternal seemingly material. What to do if your natural stone countertop has lost its luster and taken on dull colors?

The Stone to its Original Beauty

Polishing will help restore the ideal look to the stone; stone countertops often need such processing. It can be done in 2 ways:

- entrust polishing to specialists - the method requires additional financial investments but will free you from physical effort;
- polish a product made of natural stone yourself.

Self-Polishing Stone

First, I would like to make a reservation that self-polishing natural stone will only help restore beauty and brilliance. It will be difficult to independently remove cracks, chips, and other traces of mechanical damage from the stone surface. For this, it is better to contact a specialist.

Self-polishing a stone is rather long and laborious, often beyond many's power. To carry it out, you will need:

- sandpaper with different grain sizes;
- soft clothes or polishing wheels(for machining);
- special chemistry for stone
- grinding wheels (for machining
- sand.

All stone polishing is carried out in several stages:

1. Grinding - is done with different grinding wheels or sandpaper with a coarse grain (for small items). In addition, you can use sand or pumice. The stone's surface is polished to a flat horizon at this stage. On average, you will have to remove 3-4 mm. Grinding can be done both manually and using special tools, for example, an angle grinder (grinder);
2. Polishing - after grinding, the stone's surface is polished. This is done using wax or special tools, such as a stone polish. Many experts believe that it is best to use wax-based polishes. The polishing agent used is applied to the surface of the stone and rubbed with a soft cloth or polishing wheel until a shine appears;
3. Surface treatment - after polishing, it is necessary to treat the surface with protective and decorative agents. Many different substances on the market give

the natural stone the desired look. Some give the appearance of a "wet stone" or tinted effect; others emphasize the structure of the stone, highlighting its texture. When choosing such tools, you need to remember that the polishing of the stone with a paste can come to naught due to an incorrectly selected tool. Substances contained in formulations can react and damage the product itself. Try to purchase products for polishing and processing natural stones from one manufacturer.

Suppose you decide to polish your window sill or countertop made of natural stone. As a result, you will get a completely renewed product that delights you with beauty and brilliance.

Book 3
What's that Rock?

Happy people look at the sky, and sad people look at their feet. We can assure you that many people have become happier precisely because they carefully looked at their feet and did not look at the clouds. We not only urge you to follow their example but also explain what you need to pay attention to and what places to walk to find a real treasure among ordinary stones: diamonds, amber, gold, and even meteorites.

ADME draws your attention to the fact that each country's legislation restricts prospectors' activities for minerals and precious metals in different ways. Therefore, before you search, find out which finds will not violate local laws.

The Most Important Rocks to Look for

Amber

Amber 1

Where you can find it: The most affordable option is to go to the Baltic Spit. Amber is mined along the entire length of the Baltic coast in Poland and the Kaliningrad region. There are deposits in other places, such as Ukraine, the Rivne region, the Dominican Republic, and Burma. Still, only in the Baltic will you be offered an excursion that includes the collection of amber on the shore and in the quarry wasteland.

It is better to go in late autumn, winter, or early spring. After storms, the course of amber begins. Strong waves wash away the amber-bearing rock and throw ashore heaps of fin and algae, in which you have to rummage to find amber. Experienced hunters do not wait until amber is thrown onto land. They enter the icy water, fish out accumulations of fin and algae with large nets, carry the wet pile to the shore, and carefully sort it out in search of pieces of amber. It is believed that the most productive storm is short-lived because a prolonged storm will simply carry all the washed amber back to the sea, and it can only be obtained if you have a diving suit and good cold tolerance.

The most expensive and rare specimens of amber are pieces with insects, small animals, fry, blades of grass, etc., trapped millions of years ago in resin. Such inclusions are called inclusions. And the value of such finds often exceeds the value of diamonds.

meteorites

Precious stones and metals can be bought at every jewellery store. But you won't find meteorites there because they are much rarer, which means possessing them is much more pleasant. Large meteorites that form funnels fall rarely, and small ones more often. They are worth trying to find.

Where to find it: Folks who have made it their hobby to find meteorites advise beginners who have not yet acquired a metal detector to start searching from flat roofs.

Yes, it sounds strange. But the fact is that on the roof, you will not be distracted by objects of terrestrial origin, and it is there that you can find a lot of micrometeorites. Do not disregard the holes under the drains, which could get meteorite during heavy rain and water flows. Check out your finds. All meteorites have a "melting crust" - a thin layer of melted substances that make up the "guest from space" and regmaglypts - small depressions located over the entire surface of the meteorite body.

Diagnosis

Diamonds 1

If you think you're lucky, try your luck searching for the hardest mineral on our planet - diamond. However, it's not just luck, of course. Washing diamond-bearing rock in a special sieve is hard work that may not pay off. Therefore, tune in not to the discovery of the century but to an unusual adventure you will tell your best friends about for a long time.

Where to find it: The world's only diamond quarry, the Diamond Crater, open to visitors, is located in the USA, in Arkansas. Any found stone is yours. So keep your eyes always open, and don't miss the gem: it can easily mislead you with its unassuming appearance. Rough diamonds are nothing like the sparkling diamonds we see in jewellery stores.

Opals

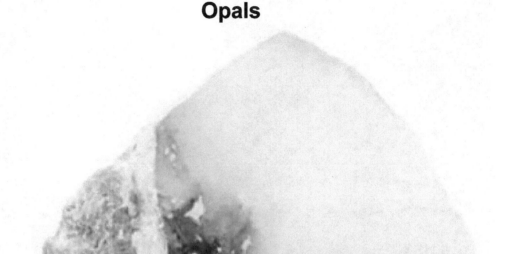

Australia beckons not only with gold. It is also famous for its opals: the most magnificent stones are mined here. As with gold, anyone can try their hand at mining. But with opals, it is more difficult because if you do not have special equipment, you will have to wander through the old tunnels, peering into the worked-out rock, hoping that those who were

Opals 1

here before you missed some good stones. However, this often happens. Opals glow in the ultraviolet, so if you take an ultraviolet

LED flashlight with you, you will not be left without a find.

Where to find it: To maximize your chances of success, head to the opal capital of the world, Coober Pedy.

Geodes

Geodes 1

If you cannot get out in search of gold and precious stones, then do not despair because even in an ordinary cobblestone at first glance, unimaginable beauty can be hidden.

Geodes are cavities in rocks, "overgrown" from the inside with crystals of such minerals as emerald, amethyst, agate, chalcedony, crystal, topaz, and opal. This is not a definitive list, but the most beautiful geodes contain these minerals. To find a geode, pay attention to rounded stones with small bumps and growths shaped like cauliflower inflorescences. They can be of any sort of size - from small pebbles to huge boulders. The most "promising" stones make a dull sound when tapped. Such stones must be split or sawn, then polished on one side to better emphasize the inner beauty of the stone.

Where to look: Everywhere

Tourmaline

What is tourmaline Tourmaline belongs to the group of aluminosilicates containing boron? Multiple metal impurities give these stones a colorful color. In the Sinhalese language, the word "tourmaline" refers to various gems, and the red gems of this group were previously called Lalas. What else should you need to know about tourmaline? For the first time, they started talking about tourmalines not so long ago. They were brought to the Netherlands from the island of Ceylon in the 18th century, where these stones have been used for more than five hundred years. European scientists later studied and evaluated the stone, discovering its amazing nature and rare beauty. According to their natural properties, the stones of the tourmaline group are very diverse, but there are common features: Crystals are shiny, transparent, or cloudy. Changes color depending on the lighting has spots of different colors. Electrified by friction, heat, and pressure. Hardness - 7.5 points out

of 10.

Tourmaline 1

The density is 3.26 g/cm³. On the site of the project "Drawing Minerals," created by a group of authors, it is said that the group of minerals, united under the name tourmaline, includes about fifteen different stones. They contain lithium, magnesium, chromium, sodium, or calcium. Such a mineral has a complex chemical formula.

Kinds of Tourmalines are divided into types: the stone's composition and color, the mineral's degree of rarity, and places of its extraction. Most of the varieties are difficult to find in their pure form, and their names are used only by gemologists - specialists involved in the definition, evaluation, and certification of precious stones. But some stones are valuable for jewelers and collectors of rare minerals. Among them, the most famous is elbaite, which has several popular varieties. The following trade names know: Rubellite is a transparent red or pink mineral. Verdelite is a transparent light green stone, the most common of the noble types. Indicolite is a translucent azure tourmaline. Achroite is a white or colorless mineral. Watermelon tourmaline is a transparent two-tone red-green stone (its varieties are "Moor's head" and "Turk's head"). Jewelers, magicians, and esotericists use schorl - opaque black tourmaline and burgherite, which has a brown color. There are adornments made of dark green chromdravite and blue deer stone. But the most valuable and desirable find for all jewelers in the world is the Paraiba tourmaline. This is the name of a very beautiful transparent turquoise crystal. It not only entered the top five most expensive gems in the world but also changed the gem market, becoming one of the most sought-after investment assets

Tourmaline 2

Tourmaline 3

Legends and Facts

Other names for the stone are "chrysolite tourmaline" from the island of Ceylon, "electric charge," "Ceylon magnet," and "dust-catching stone."

It is called the main sensation of the last century.

Today's largest tourmaline is the "Divine Ethereal Carolina Paraiba," weighing almost 192 carats.

It became part of a piece of jewelry of incredible beauty and was in the private collection of Vincent Bush until 2014 and was later put up for auction.

The largest tourmaline is listed in the Guinness Book of Records. The mineral was awarded the Nobel Prize thanks to the work of Pierre Curie.

Deposits And Value of The Natural Stone

The United States ranks first in the extraction of tourmalines. A valuable mineral is mined in many countries, but expensive types of tourmaline are not found everywhere. Where's it obtained, and how's it used? The largest deposits of amazing stone are located in: China, Myanmar, and Sri Lanka; India and on the island of Madagascar; Canada, Brazil, and the USA; South Africa, Angola, and Mozambique; Australia; Italy and Switzerland; Afghanistan and Tajikistan; Russia. Natural tourmalines are durable, cool to the touch, and heterogeneous in structure and color. Chemists have learned how to synthesize tourmalines in the laboratory for industrial applications. The stone is used in radio engineering and medicine (for medical equipment), and natural gems have become a piece of valuable jewelry and ornamental stone. Price Tourmaline is considered a gemstone of the third order (in value), along with minerals such as spinel, opal, topaz, and aquamarine. Some types of tourmalines are very expensive (Paraiba tourmaline), and some are cheaper because they are more common in nature. Inexpensive stones include green translucent varieties of the mineral. Jewelers prefer stones weighing at least 2 carats of rare species. Jewelry brand Tiffany & Co has entered into a contract with Brazilian mining companies to buy back all tourmalines, as they are found less and less. Therefore, the value of the stone is constantly increasing. So, for example, a ring with natural Paraiba tourmaline costs more than $1 million. The cost of popular tourmalines up to 5 mm in size is $10-100. The price of rare species and large specimens grows by 20% annually and is calculated individually.

How to care for tourmaline products Unusual stone jewelry requires delicate handling, regardless of its value:

Wipe the products with a soft cloth dampened with water, as the stone attracts small dust particles. Do not utilize steam or ultrasonic cleaners to avoid damaging the stone. Wash jewelry with warm water and mild soap using a soft sponge. Then rinse the product with water to remove soap stains. Remove jewelry when doing household chores. Store them in a box with soft sides and a lid, wrapped in a soft cloth. Remember the value of a unique stone and treat it with care. Tourmaline in magic, astrology, and healing It is often called the "stone of poets," as tourmaline reveals the gift of poetry and writing in people. Many poems and books have been written about it; what other magical properties does the amazing mineral that has conquered the world have? magical properties.

The book by Alexandra Cherepanova, "The Magical Properties of Stones for Magicians," describes the unique properties of natural tourmaline, which were known to adherents of magical teachings. The mysterious Cleopatra gave the red tourmaline to Julius Caesar because she believed that the stone could recognize any lie, see through walls and distances, and bring the owner success and well-deserved fame. Cleopatra's tourmaline passed from Caesar to Charlemagne, from him to the Templars, to the Swedes, and with them came Russia. The stone looked like a pink vine and was presented to Catherine II by the Swedish king. It is believed that tourmalines kindle love and passion and develop self-confidence in people. They also teach you to think rationally, draw the right conclusions, and help you quickly concentrate and achieve complete harmony. Healing amulets from tourmaline Karen Frezier, author of Crystals.

Practical guide: how to choose, feel, use, advises using the energy of tourmaline for relieving nervous and muscle tension, ensuring healthy sleep; improving blood circulation and cleansing blood vessels from blood clots and cholesterol plaques; normalization of the work of the genital organs and the endocrine system; improve metabolism; prevention and treatment of osteochondrosis and intervertebral hernias. Here is how tourmalines of different colors work: Blue stone relieves headaches and benefits vision. The green mineral fights chronic and acute diseases of the liver and gallbladder. Alternative medicine indicates the ability of the stone to regenerate body cells using infrared radiation. Crushed to a powder, tourmaline warms the joints, bones, spine, and sore muscles. Thus it is possible to ionize the air.

Shale
Shale Identification

SHALE is a very common type of foliated metamorphic rock. It is made up of visible mineral grains in the form of sheets.

It typically forms on the continental side of a converging plate boundary where sedimentary rocks, such as shales, have been subjected to compressive and temperature forces. Under these conditions, the clay minerals of the sedimentary rocks are transformed into laminated metamorphic minerals such as muscovite, biotite, and chlorite.

To become a shale, a shale will first become a shale to continue to become a phyllite, and then if conditions continue to increase, it will become a shale. If the shale is further subjected to metamorphism, it could become a granular rock known as gneiss.

A schist rock does not need a specific mineral composition to be called a "schist." It only needs to contain enough aligned lamellar metamorphic minerals to exhibit a foliation with visible grains. This texture allows the rock to break into thin plates along the direction of alignment of the laminated mineral grains. This type of rock weakness is known as schistosity.

Sometimes, the laminated minerals may be graphite, talc, or hornblende from carbonaceous, basaltic, or other sources.

Shale 1

As explained above, mica minerals such as chlorite, muscovite, and biotite are the most characteristic minerals in shale.

These were formed through the metamorphism of clay minerals present in the protolith. Other minerals in shale include quartz and feldspar, which are inherited from the protolith. Micas, feldspars, and quartz typically represent the majority of minerals present in shale rock.

Shales are often named according to the naked-eye minerals of metamorphic origin that are obvious and abundant when the rock is examined.

For example, muscovite schist when muscovite predominates or chlorite schist when chlorite is abundant. Likewise, biotite schist, kyanite schist, garnet schist, staurolite schist, hornblende schist, graphite schist, etc., are also common.

Sometimes they are named after two minerals; the first refers to the less abundant mineral and the second to the more abundant mineral. For example, garnet graphite schist.

Shale Properties
Metamorphic Rock-Petrographic Description Shale

Rock name	Shale
Color	Green to gray
Texture	Schistose
Structure	Foliate
Minerals	Sericite, chlorite, biotite, graphite, garnet, hornblende, kyanite
Degree of deformation	S 1
Type of metamorphism	Middle-grade regional
Protolith	Pelitic

Shale Formation

Shale is a rock that has been exposed to a moderate level of temperature and a moderate level of pressure. Its formation is from its protoliths, commonly in sedimentary rocks such as shale. In the vicinity of converging plate boundaries, heat and chemical activity transform shale clay minerals into mica minerals (flaky minerals), such as muscovite, biotite, and chlorite. The directed pressure pushes the transforming clay minerals from their random orientations into a common parallel alignment, where the long axes of the laminated minerals are oriented perpendicular to the direction of the compressive force.

Shale Uses

Shale is not particularly used in industry due to its low strength. However, it may contain semi-precious stones such as garnets, sapphire, scapolite, ruby, kyanite, tanzanite, andalusite, emerald, sphene, and chrysoberyl.

Where to find: Russia, China, Argentina, Libya, and the United States.

Shale 2

Anorthosite

Anorthosite. Igneous rock, of solidified magma, a multiphase sample of high temperature, composed of molten rock (mainly silicates) and gases, uncommon on our planet, although abundant on the surface of the Moon.

Description And Composition

Anorthosite has a whitish or grayish coloration, medium or coarse grain, and is formed by feldspar(minerals) rich-in calcium and plagioclase.

Anorthosite is an igneous rock composed of 90% or more calcic plagioclase. Its name comes from anorthosite, an old name for plagioclase that has also given its name to anorthite, a specific variety of plagioclase.

Light areas on the Moon's surface correspond to anorthosite fields and have been the subject of many studies.

Anorthosites are also common in stratified intrusions on Earth. Anorthosite from stratified intrusions can form as cumulus layers in the upper parts of the intrusion or by intrusion into a stratified intrusion shortly before it fully crystallizes.

Terrestrial anorthosite arose in Precambrian times; its approximate age is approximately 4.5 billion years.

Where to find: Anorthosite has been found in eastern North America, southern Africa, and some specific points, such as the Magis White Caves in Gudvangen (Norway).

Agate

Agate is a variety of chalcedony. It belongs to the trigonal crystallization system, is of volcanic origin, and owes its color to the multiple inclusions deposited during its growth.

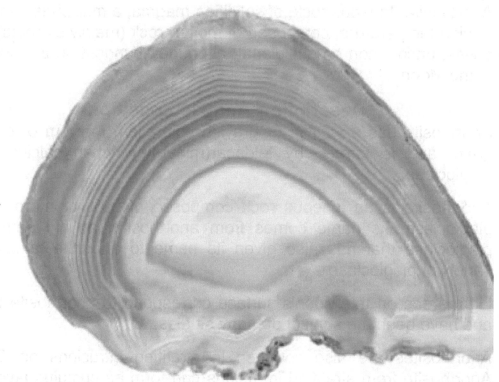

Once a section of agate is polished, we can appreciate its growth by the different circumcentre lines that we find, which are the different layers of inclusions that give it different colors. Agate bowls can be hollow inside, being able to crystallize quartz or amethyst in the central part.

Etymology

The name Agata originates from the Achates river (Sicily), where it was found for the first time.

Agate mineralogy

PHYSICAL PROPERTIES

- Group silicates - tectosilicates
- Composition sio2 _
- Color colorless, white, yellow, grey, brown, blue, or red
- Crystal system hexagonal / trigonal
- Crystal habit cryptocrystalline
- Hardness 7
- Conchoidal fracture
- Exfoliation none
- Gloss vitreous to cerulean
- White stripe
- Transparency from translucent to opaque
- Specific gravity 2.7
- Refractive index 1.53 - 1.54

Therapeutic Properties

Agate is considered a soft energy stone is known to bring harmony and balance. It promotes self-confidence and concentration and favors spiritual growth, love, and courage.

Agate is slightly protective when it is dark. At a curative level, it is said that placed on the forehead calms fever, and placed along the legs helps to eliminate liquids. Moss agate and dendritic agate varieties are often used on plants to promote growth and health.

Mineralogical Characteristics

Agate is a microcrystalline variety of the quartz group, a type of chalcedony of various colors that usually has chromatic bands. There are several kinds of agates, and their color depends on the different materials they may contain. The most abundant is gray, although we also find them in yellow, orange, white, blue, brown, and pink. Being a porous mineral, it can sometimes be dyed with bright colors, as in the case of fuchsia agate, intense blue agate, or dark green agate.

Agate, in its natural state, usually occurs in the form of inclusions within ovoid or spherical cavities of volcanic rocks. When an agate geode is opened, quartz, amethyst, or calcite crystallization usually appears inside.

Where to find: Brazil, Uruguay, Argentina, China, India, Madagascar, Morocco, the Czech Republic, and the United States.

Amethyst

Amethyst has been widely known for thousands of years; since ancient Egypt, it has been used to create jewelry, personal seals, and carvings. In the Middle Ages, Christianity used amethyst as a sign of renunciation of worldly goods and chastity. It is still worn nowadays as part of rings by many cardinals and bishops. Amethyst also symbolized divine wisdom.

Etymology

The word "Amethyst" comes from the Greek name "amethystos," that means sober because it was used as an antidote to drunkenness.

Amethyst mineralogy

- Hardness: 7
- Colour: Purple
- The Stripe: White
- Luster: Vitreous
- Fracture: Conchoidal

Where to find: The most important deposits are in Brazil, Uruguay, Mozambique, Mexico, Bolivia, Zambia, Namibia, South Africa, and the Russian Urals. We can find it in several locations in Spain, giving the best specimens of the Montseny massif between Barcelona and Girona.

New Age Properties of Amethyst

Amethyst is a really powerful and protecting stone. Natural tranquilizer that helps block negative environmental energies. Meditating helps you keep your thoughts away from the mundane, promoting the assimilation of new ideas. It provides common sense, enhances memory and motivation, and centers you emotionally.

Amethyst 1

On a healing level, amethyst is ideal for relieving the pain of physical, emotional, and psychological tensions, blocking geopathic stress. Fights insomnia and provides restful sleep. She connects the physical, mental, and emotional bodies with the spiritual. She cleanses the aura, transmutes negative energy, and stimulates the throat and crown chakras. Use a point; put it facing you if you want it to absorb energy or the other way around if you want to eliminate it. Under the pillow in case you want to improve sleep quality.

Jade

The jade stone has great symbology and is considered a sacred stone in China. Its name dates back to the time of the conquest of the Americas and comes from "piedra de Tejada" (colic stone), although throughout history, it has also been known as "kidney stone."

The green Jade stone symbolizes the Yang, a stone with solar, imperial, and indestructible qualities. Hence the importance it has in China and Central America, where it has an important funerary role in addition to its spiritual or healing properties.

The prestigious Chinese thinker Confucius stated that men should try to have the properties of the Jade stone, which has the five cardinal virtues: wisdom, love, justice, courage, and modesty.

Jade is composed of silicate mineral particles distributed in a structure of very fine granules and intertwined fibers that give it high strength and durability. A completely opaque stone, which is impenetrable to light.

Jade 1

History Of Jade Stone

The Jade stone is closely linked to the culture of China. It has a great influence throughout Southeast Asia, called the "Gem of Heaven," since it was associated with immortality and the power to create a bridge between the sky and Earth.

Considered a real gem, the green Jade stone began to be extracted more than 6,000 years ago, and it is necessary to differentiate between the two varieties.

On the one hand, there is Jadeite, a group of alkaline pyroxenes, and on the other, Nephritis, a group of amphiboles. Both were called Jade until 1863, when Alexis Damour, a mineralogist of French origin, discovered that although they had similar properties and appearance, they came from different minerals.

Jade Stone Properties

The properties of the Jade stone are innumerable, both at a spiritual and healing level, which is why alchemists related it to the philosopher's stone, a symbol of immortality.

- Spiritual properties of Jade:

One of the properties of green Jade is that it improves people's emotional state and is associated with the fourth chakra, which is related to emotional health. It is said that it favors love in a person, reduces irritability, and emits calming energy that favors meditation.

- Healing properties of Jade stone:

When talking about the Jade stone and its benefits, it should be noted that it helps the kidneys and the adrenal glands and cleanses toxins, increasing defense mechanisms and accelerating the healing of stitches.

It is also said to encourage fertility and aid in childbirth, calming the nervous system and channeling passion in constructive ways.

It helps us raise our consciousness since it is a balancing and stabilizing stone for emotions, preventing them from controlling us. It also favors the balance between the emotional and intellectual aspects, and its energy favors a state of serenity, helping to remember dreams and interpret them.

Thanks to the balance, it is very effective in times of stress and exhaustion, especially when they come from unfavorable environmental energies.

Symbology and meaning of the Jade stone

The Jade stone has a great connection with the heart, the feminine, the planet Venus and water, and it is a gem that is studied in depth in gem therapy (a science dedicated to the study of stones) since, according to this Kind of science, it's a cleanser, a nerve toner and helps release tension.

One of the benefits of Jade stone is that it balances and calms the nervous system and reinforces the immune system, in addition to many others.

As for the symbology of the Jade stone, in Central America, it symbolizes the soul, the spirit, the heart, or the core of a being. In Egypt, it was a healing stone with great value. The Armenians, Arabs, and Turks, since 4000 BC, have used it as an amulet.

In short, Jade is a beautiful, mystical, precious gem that has fascinated different cultures throughout history.

Green jade has a very deep esoteric meaning. Hence it is a symbol of purity, wisdom, and serenity and one of the most valued minerals.

Jade 2

Jade Stone Colors

Although the green Jade stone is the most popular, the truth is that the shades of Jade are very varied, and beyond many ranges of green, we can find red, yellow, white, brown, black, blue, pink, and lavender Jade.

Green jade analogies and universal symbols that unite gods and men coexist like a kind of bridge. Depending on the tonality of the gem, some qualities or others are intensely attributed to it.

How to Use Jade Stone?

What is Jade stone used for? You should know that it is a stone widely used in meditation and as an amulet.

Although without a doubt, the most widespread use is Jade stone jewelry, which has been used for over 5000 years since they were considered amulets that attracted luck.

Where to find: Myanmar, New Zealand, Canada, Taiwan, Guyana, Surinam, southern Europe, Russia, and China.

Baryta

Baryta 1

Physical Properties

- Group sulfates
- Composition base 4
- Color colorless, white, grey, bluish, greenish, beige
- Rhombic crystalline system
- Crystalline habits from tabular to prismatic
- Hardness 3 - 3.5
- Unequal fracture
- Perfect exfoliation
- Gloss vitreous, resinous, pearly
- White stripe
- Transparency from transparent to translucent
- Specific gravity 4.5
- Refractive index 1.63 - 1.65

Mineralogical Characteristics

Barite is the most common barium ore and its main ore.

Its name comes from the Greek "barys," which means "heavy," due to its high specific weight. It is also called "heavy spar."

Barite usually crystallizes in tabular, colorful, or " cockscomb " aggregates. It can also be found fibrous, massive, stalactitic, or concretionary. Rosette-shaped barium crystals are called desert roses.

Baryta 2

Barite is a common secondary mineral in lead and zinc seams or sedimentary rocks such as limestone, marine deposits, and igneous rock cavities. It is soft and fragile, so it is not used for carving.

Deposits: Spain, France, Romania, Great Britain, Germany, India, and the United States.

Therapeutic Properties

Barite helps to cleanse and rebalance the chakras. It enhances one's autonomy, communication, understanding between people, and overcoming shyness. It facilitates memory, motivation, and vitality.

It is said to calm the digestive and nervous systems physically.

Epidote
Physical Properties

- Group silicates - sorosilicates
- Composition ca 2 al 2 (fe, al)(sio 4)(si 2 o 7)o(oh)
- Color pistachio green
- Monoclinic crystalline system
- Crystal habit short to long prismatic
- Hardness 6 - 7
- Fracture uneven to splintery
- Exfoliation good
- Vitreous gloss
- Stripe colorless to greyish
- Transparency translucent
- Specific gravity 3.4
- Refractive index 1.74 - 1.78

Mineralogical Characteristics

The name epidote comes from the Greek "epidosis," which means "increase" since it always has one of the sides of the prisms greater than the rest.

Deposits: United States, Bulgaria, Austria, France, Russia, Norway, South Africa, Pakistan, Mozambique, and Mexico.

Therapeutic Properties

Epidote is considered a transformative and healing stone for the emotional body. It helps to release pain and connect with personal power, sense of identity, and enjoyment of life in a realistic way, dispelling excessive self-criticism.

Epidote 1

On a physical level, it is said that the epidote regulates the nervous and immune systems and provides vigor and cell regeneration. Benefits the brain, thyroid, liver, gallbladder, and adrenal glands.

Stibnite

Stibnite is a rock extracted from antimony, which is why it is so important because it is a widely used element in industries. The main sectors dedicated to medicine, technology, and metallurgy are the ones that make the most use of Stibnite. It should be noted that it is a toxic and very strange metal.

This mineral has non-metallic and metallic properties; It is important to highlight that its abundance in the Earth's crust is very low; it is also considered a stable element; that is, it does not dissolve in alkaline acids, nor is it a conductor of electricity or heat.

Its appearance is quite particular; for that reason, it usually stands out among other stones. Its brightness, size, sharpness, and shape are the ones that attract the most attention. Despite having a resistant appearance, due to its color being very similar to metal, this mineral is fragile but a bit heavy and soft in texture. This rock sometimes has an opaque surface but with certain metallic sparkles, and its colors always range from black to lead grey.

When Stibnite is exposed to the elements, its surface tends to darken, and this is due to the oxidation process that the stone undergoes, just as if it were an apple cut in half. This reaction occurs when the antinomies are transformed; this mineral is associated with pyrite, galena, marcasite, barite, calcite, pyrite, and other stones.

History of the Stibnite

Stibnite comes from the Greek "time," and the Latin "stibium" was given to it because Dioscorides and the old Pliny mentioned it after studying its mineral composition. These two words are responsible for describing the metallic aspect that the stone has, and it is for this cause that they also gave it the pseudonym "antimonite."

In ancient times the Stibnite was discovered; it is still unknown exactly in what century the Stibnite was sighted for the first time, but what can be admitted is that it occurred at a time when the traditions were very different from those of today.

Some legends say that the people who worked in a mine in the town of Hidalgo were the ones who first found the mineral, and after extracting it and taking it home, the benefits it attracted were multiple.

Stibnite 1

Origin and Formation of Stibnite

It should be noted that this stone only forms in low-temperature hydrothermal veins, where the environment only reaches between 50 and 200°C; however, it is also possible that they form in chemical deposits associated with hydrothermal vents.

A Stibnite stone is rarely formed by the recrystallization of a mineral or by the chemical transformation of limestone rocks. Being a metal, this stone is associated with gold, lead, silver, and cinnabar, among others.

Physical Characteristics of Stibnite

Stibnite is a metal extracted from antimony, which also falls within the group of sulfides because it is only found in compact groups. It is common for this stone to appear twisted, with vertical or folded grooves and in a metallic, lead-gray color. Some specimens have bluish and iridescent reflections, especially when they show alterations.

Unlike other stones, Stibnite can bend and be flexible; if you want to mold it at any time, its final shape will remain forever. As we mentioned before, this mineral is soft but heavy, and it is easy to exfoliate if it has to be done in the direction in which the crystal elongations are found.

Stibnite is so fragile that it only ranks number 2 on the Mohs scale. Due to its opaque appearance, light cannot pass through the mineral. This rock, when reduced, becomes a white powder with hydrochloric acid. By approaching a match or a candle, you can see how the Stibnite melts.

External causes can alter this stone; in its place, kermesite is born, a mineral very similar to Stibnite but has reddish tones. It should be noted that this rock tends to be confused with bismuthinite. Still, the only way to differentiate them is when weighing them and studying them very well because the latter has small yellowish crystals, and its melting is slow.

Deposits of the Stibnite

The main deposit where the Stibnite can be found is on the island of Shikoku, Japan; for a moment; this location became very famous for the wonderful specimens obtained, in addition to the sizes and groupings of the Stibnite stones that were extracted from the place were incomparable.

However, another very important deposit is that of Xikuangshan, Hunan province, but we cannot leave behind the mine of Wuning, Qingjiang, Dahegou, and Lushi, among others. But it should be noted that specimens of Stibnite are produced in this way in Romania and some deposits in Slovakia, Australia, Serbia, Peru, Bolivia and Mexico, Austria, the Czech Republic, Germany, Spain, Italy, and Morocco.

Stibnite 2

General Properties of Stibnite

- It should be noted that Stibnite is a stone that works on the mental and physical plane of people. Next, we will mention some benefits that it attracts:
- It is responsible for promoting a general and profound change in people.
- It allows individuals to have enough self-confidence and feel that their self-esteem is high.
- The Stibnite works as a protective amulet because it is responsible for protecting and cleaning all the negative energies that surround the person who possesses it.
- This crystal is responsible for amplifying positive energies.
- At the same time, it permits the people who wear it to gather courage and maintain contact with an entity from another world.
- It is perfect for the ones who want to protect themselves from possession and attachment.
- Stibnite is a stone that helps improve blood circulation.
- In addition, it calms stomach pains and reduces problems related to the digestive system.
- Stibnite is a stone that helps to face sudden changes.
- Enhance harsh environments and allow chaos to become order.
- It is a useful rock during meditation and sessions that help you release stress.
- It allows the body to support the energy changes occasionally experienced efficiently.
- It is very easy to eliminate toxins from the body and all the things causing damage to the body.

Uses of Stibine

- Stibnite is a rock with multiple uses; although it is not widely used in jewelry, it is very commonly used in other areas.
- Collectors, especially the larger specimens, highly value this stone.
- It is common to find traces of Stibnite in glasses since most are made from this rock.
- Some ancient civilizations used this stone as a cosmetic; in this way, it gave them a metallic style.
- Fireworks and buckshot contain antimony, a mineral that contains Stibnite.
- The electrical industries use this rock to make batteries and infrared detectors.
- Meanwhile, in textiles, a knob of Stibnite is usually added for impregnations and alloys and is anti-flammable.
- In addition to metals (e.g. silver and steel) most mechanical tools also have a little Stibnite.
- It should also be noted that Stibnite is used to make some electrical appliances such as electric stoves, blenders, or toasters.

Curious Facts About Stibnite

- In Roman times, some used crushed Stibnite to make up their eyes.

- Some stories have detailed that Stibnite caused the death of many people; this is because the correct use of the mineral was unknown. For this reason, before using one of these stones or touching any sample, it is best to be very careful when handling Stibnite.

- It is not recommended to be exposed for so long to Stibnite, nor keep it close to your body because it can cause annoying symptoms such as headaches, dizziness, and nausea, among other conditions.

- Most of the cosmetics that were made in the past had a small amount of Stibnite, which was obtained naturally.

- During the Middle Ages and the Renaissance, Stibnite was also used for pharmaceutical purposes, especially by alchemists.

- It is said that, in first times, they made antimony cups which, when the wine was poured into it, acted on the tartaric acid of the wine and the antimony of the cup, which caused an emetic effect in everyone who drank from it.

- Stibnite is a really useful stone, but it is not recommended to wear for a long time because it has been studied and proven to cause some health complications.

Sometimes Gems Fall from The Sky

However, sometimes you don't need to look for treasures. They will find you falling on their heads from the sky, as happened in Hawaii in early June 2018, during the eruption of the Kilauea volcano. A sharp and powerful ejection of lava caused the surroundings to fall asleep with small green olivine crystals. Usually, olivines are found inside lava flows, but during sharp eruptions of lava, such an interesting anomaly can be observed.

Today, thousands of people world-wide, of all ages and social positions, collect minerals. It is difficult to know the number of fans of this science throughout the world, but there may be more than 100,000 people in Europe and many more in the United States of America. Possibly in the rest of the world, there is a similar figure. The number of collectors grows every year. It extends not only in the most developed countries, but important collections also appear in developing countries or countries with emerging economies.

The way to obtain the pieces of the collections is very varied. First, collectors can obtain them from their collection in the field or the mines. The profile of the mineral collector in developed countries is that of a person who does this work as a hobby during leisure hours and classifies and prepares samples in his spare time.

Many collectors also obtain samples through exchanges of their pieces with other collectors or, very commonly, through purchase. This purchase can be made directly from miners or other collectors but is almost always made through retail purchases at small specialty stores, mineral fairs, or over the Internet.

Because of this, a certain mineral market has been generated, currently very globalized, with tens of thousands of people living directly or indirectly from it.

The high demand for collectible minerals raises the possibility that more samples will be sought and extracted in other parts where sensitivity to this market has not yet emerged. Indeed, this demand makes it easier for small communities to find additional sources of income from marketing local mineral products. This type of extraction is, by definition, artisanal, which is why it would most likely not be profitable for traditional mining companies, but only for micro-enterprises.

On the other hand, it's crucial to remember that the collected minerals can be given two types of added value:

(1) A preparation to highlight the most interesting aspects of the specimen

(2) A stoning or carving to make ornamental objects. Or jewelry.

In developing countries, harvesting can be a mechanism for developing small micro-enterprises in rural areas. However, this type of resource and how to carry out the related tasks are generally unknown in these countries. On the other hand, in some countries where collectible minerals are already traded, there is often a lack of criteria for valuing the pieces correctly or how to treat them correctly during the collection, cleaning, storage, or export processes. This entails the deterioration of the pieces and, therefore, the reduction of their value.

The key goal of this work is to provide these small communities with the basic knowledge to collect, conserve and market minerals for collection.

Today, the jewelry industry has reached such a level that fashionable and beautiful products are made from almost any material. Habitual precious stones often fade into the background, giving way to more budgetary semi-precious and ornamental stones. But by no means do all customers know how the inserts differ and why prices vary so much for minerals that look similar in appearance. To understand this, let's make a short excursion into the history of the jewelry industry and consider each type of insert separately. Gems are The most expensive and most valuable inserts. What is the reason for the high cost of such minerals? Let's figure it out in order. The first thing to consider is that gems are natural minerals formed complexly in the Earth's crust. Accordingly, a gem can only be called such if it is rare in nature.

Here are some statistics from world practice. The relative cost of extraction of the most expensive stones as a percentage of the cost of total production at the beginning of the 21st century was as follows:

- Emeralds - 43,
- Rubies - 14,
- Opals - 10,
- Sapphires - 6,
- Jadeite - 6,
- Turquoise - 5,
- Other colored stones - 16%.

This shows that the high cost of precious stones is due, first of all, to the complexity of their extraction.

What other indicators can reveal a gem among all the others?
Hardness. The mineral should not be exposed to external influences - scratch and chip.

In Russia, following the Federal Law "On Precious Metals and Precious Stones," this list includes natural diamonds, emeralds, rubies, sapphires, alexandrites, and pearls. Unique amber formations are also equated to precious stones. From here, we see that its high cost is quite understandable. In addition, a significant role in determining the price of a product is played by the degree of its fashionability.

Simply put, the more an accessory fall under the definition of a "fashion trend," the higher its cost. The world of precious stones is large and confusing, especially when viewed superficially. At the moment, more than 2.5 thousand minerals are known, but only a little more than a hundred are of value in the jewelry industry and arts and crafts. It is quite difficult to understand the intricacies of varieties of precious, semi-precious, and ornamental stones, but there are also valuable natural formations that are not minerals. Therefore, within the framework of this publication, several approaches to the classification of valuable minerals and natural formations will be considered. What are the types of gems? The names of the precious stones and minerals (which are the same) are presented differently in various classifications since a unified system has not yet been developed. From the generally accepted point of view, only the most beautiful, rare, and expensive minerals and other natural formations can be considered precious stones.

According to Article 1 of the Federal Law of March 26, 1998 No. 41-FZ, diamonds, rubies, emeralds, alexandrites, and sapphires, as well as natural pearls of natural origin, that is, organic, are exclusively precious stones. This also sometimes includes amber, but in the presence of some unique features - special inclusions, heavyweight, and so on. Ring from the collection "Diamonds of Yakutia" in Sunlight However, there are nuances here, too: gems in jewelry look very impressive and cost accordingly. But very small or defective minerals lose a lot of value, while semi-precious gems of large sizes and rare colors can be equated in value with precious stones of the first order.

Top 10 Popular Gemstones Considering gems in terms of popularity is not very correct because the rarer the mineral, the more valuable it is. Therefore, here we will rely on the popularity of names and the value of noble minerals, not their actual popularity among consumers. Not everyone can afford a five-carat diamond ring or emerald earrings, but this does not mean they would not be desirable. Especially the beautiful ladies!

Here is a non-exhaustive list of precious and semi-precious stones, among which there are both relatively cheap and exclusive minerals.

Moonstone

Meet one of the rather rare representatives of potassium and calcium feldspars, very beloved by collectors and jewelers. The largest deposit of moonstones is being developed in Sri Lanka; in Russia, they are mined in the Urals and the vicinity of Lake Baikal. The mysterious radiance of this stone gives it a very mysterious look and attractive exterior. Moonstone (adularia) in the classic version has a milky bluish color with beautiful tints, but sunny yellowish belamorites and black adularia are also known. They are not cut. Otherwise, they lose the lion's share of their attractiveness.

Moonstone 1

This mineral has a particularly pronounced feminine energy - the Moon is favorable to the fair sex and creative individuals, regardless of gender. It is believed that the Moonstone can enhance intuition and extrasensory abilities, help in matters of the heart and correct the state of health. Moonstone has been recognized as the official gemstone of the state of Florida, even though it is not mined there.

This happened in 1970, when an American space expedition landed on the Moon, starting from a cosmodrome in Florida.

Topaz

It is difficult for an amateur to immediately recognize topaz in a stone: this mineral is too diverse in color. The most widespread are cheap colorless specimens (pure aluminum silicates). However, there are even polychrome crystals, that is, combining several shades. The diversity of topaz attracts the good eyes of jewelers to it. Topaz has another significant plus - it is very hard (8 points on the Mohs Scale), yielding only diamond and precious corundum (sapphire and ruby) in this nomination. It is chemical resistant and elegantly transparent.

Topaz 1

Despite the wide distribution (found whole crystals weighing 60-80 kg are known), pure transparent topazes of fantasy natural shades are highly valued by jewelers. And simpler options are available to absolutely everyone - such a handsome democrat.

Pomegranate

Pomegranate 1

Blood-red stones were once called Lala, without any distinction between their chemical composition and physical properties. Now only pyropes and almandines are called pomegranates; in the classic version, they resemble grains of the fruit of the same name in color. There are a lot of pomegranates with different formulas and properties in modern classification. The majority of them belong to the group of semi-precious (jewelry) stones. Some of them are not red at all!

Opal

Opals 2

As mentioned above, the once amorphous silicas, now known as opals, were valuable. They were extremely rare, which is why they often adorn the crowns of European monarchs. After the discovery of large deposits in Australia, where about 97% of opals are now mined, these stones have become much more affordable in terms of prices. It is customary to distinguish noble (precious) and ordinary (semi-precious) opals.

The former is characterized by an iridescent play of colors, transparency, or clarity and is very expensive. Minerals of saturated colors are especially highly valued - fiery, blue, and even almost black.

Pearl

The most expensive and popular precious stone of organic origin is pearls. Moreover, the most valuable is sea pearls, grown naturally in a wild pearl shell, and natural "houses" of other mollusks. A foreign body (for example, a grain of sand) gets into the shells and envelops them with a layer of mother-of-pearl. Freshwater pearls are much less valued - they resemble bumpy grains of rice and rarely have an impeccably spherical or pear-shaped shape. Cultured pearls stand apart: a foreign body is specially planted in the shell, and the mollusk completes the rest.

Pearl 1

The main criterion for the value of a pearl is its size, brilliance, and surface cleanliness. There are pearls of various shades - from white and yellowish to pink and even black (a huge rarity!). By the way, this is the only gem that is not processed. Alexandrite Before us is one of the "youngest" minerals described only in 1842. At first, a strange stone was mistaken for a not too pure emerald, but it showed slightly different physical characteristics, particularly greater hardness. The new stone was named in honor of the future Emperor Alexander II. This mineral has a great property: it changes color depending on the lighting and in the widest range: from blue-green to red-violet tones. The higher the contrast of the color change, the more valuable the stone. There are alexandrites with opal radiance.

Sapphire

The most valuable sapphire is a classic blue variety of corundum. The cheapest gem of all sapphires is an alternatively colored mineral. Geologists call only blue corundums, sapphires, and jewelers - everything except those painted in red, that is, rubies. The mineral's bright blue color is most highly valued, closer to pure cornflower blue: the darker or lighter the stone, the worse. The so-called star-shaped sapphires are interesting: under certain lighting, it seems that a six- or even a twelve-pointed star is burning inside the stone. They are not even subjected to classical cutting but are inserted into jewelry in the form of cabochons.

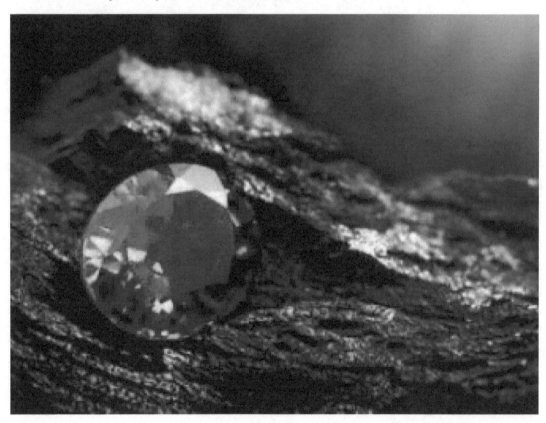

There are deposits of blue sapphires in many countries, including Russia (in the Urals and the Kola Peninsula).

Ruby

Ruby 1

Before us is a close relative of sapphire - also corundum, but blood-red in color, provided by chromium impurities. The brighter the color, the more valuable the stone, but much depends on its purity and size. Ruby is a true gemstone with a long and glorious history. Jewelry with yahonts (rubies and sapphires) was found during excavations of Etruscan burial grounds. They were known by the ancient Indians and considered the most powerful talismans, appreciated by the ancient Greeks and Romans. Rubies are described in the Bible and mentioned in the writings of Pliny.

Emerald

The ancient name of this mineral from the vast beryl family is smaragd. The flawless emerald is a transparent stone of rich green color, and the deeper the green, the better. Unfortunately, this noble mineral is very prone to cracking, which is why it is highly valued. A pure five-carat emerald is worth more than a flawless diamond of the same weight! The purity of most natural emeralds is clouded by inclusions of air and all kinds of impurities, so they are often subjected to refining (oiling).

The lion's share of the world's emerald production comes from Colombia, but minerals mined in Brazil, Afghanistan, and Zambia are of higher quality and purity. In Russia, these magnificent stones are mined mainly in the Urals. Even though emeralds were known to the ancient Egyptians, they were brought to Europe only by the conquistadors, the conquerors of the New World. By the way, they have long been considered witch stones because of their piercing green color. However, the Arabs revered emeralds and wore them as amulets, and in Russia, they were considered gems of wisdom and composure.

Diamond

Oddly enough, the standard hard diamond is a close relative of soft graphite: it also consists of pure carbon. A cut diamond is called a brilliant. It is rightfully considered the most famous and expensive gemstone. Diamonds are used not only in the jewelry industry: they are indispensable in producing cutting and drilling tools, lasers, watches, and quantum computers. A cut diamond should ideally be transparent, with a characteristic radiance and brilliance. A clean diamond is easy to lose in a glass container filled with water - it is simply invisible. Often, diamonds contain impurities that give them different shades. Some (yellow and brown) reduce the value of stones, while others (blue and pink) raise it to sky-high heights.

Diamond deposits have been found on all continents, including Antarctica. They occur in the so-called kimberlite pipes. The largest, cleanest, and most expensive diamonds are mined in Africa: Botswana, Angola, and Namibia. Russian diamond deposits are located mainly in the Urals and Yakutia.

The Most Expensive Gems

We will not repeat the above: the most expensive in ranking precious stones by value is the last five positions described above. These are gemstones of the first order and the highest value by any classification. But you need to understand that it is impossible to compile an objective list of stones by value: the cost of a carat of a mineral depends not only on its chemical formula but also on purity, transparency, size, color, presence/absence of defects, and other parameters. Therefore, this nomination presents the rarest and most expensive minerals that surpass the generally accepted standards.

So, here is a list of truly unique stones valued at fortunes:

- Tsavorite

Jewelry garnet yellowish-green. A carat costs about 3-5 thousand US dollars. Sapphire. An unheated stone of pure blue is estimated at a minimum of 4.5-6 thousand dollars/carat.

Tsavorite 1

- Red
spinel.

It is seen as one of the fastest growing minerals in price: the cost is 6-8 thousand dollars per carat. Demantoid. Another green garnet, but a pure piercing color. Ural demantoid costs about 10 thousand dollars/carat. Paraiba.

Neon blue tourmaline that glows in the dark.

Stones of average quality go for 8-12 thousand dollars/carat.

Red spinel 1

- Emerald.

Flawless, pure emeralds are extremely rare. The cost of a carat of high-quality unoiled emerald starts from 10-13 thousand dollars

Padparadscha. Sapphire of incredible orange-pink color. Cost - 10-12 thousand dollars / carat.

- Alexandrite.

The price of this stone fluctuates around 10-37 thousand dollars/carat. The most expensive is mined in Russia.

- Ruby.

A large pure stone of the top color "pigeon blood" is estimated at 15-25 thousand dollars/carat.

Jade.

The rarest transparent Jadeite, known as "imperial," costs at least 20 thousand dollars/carat.

- Diamond.

The cost of a quality colorless diamond is about $15,000/per carat. A blue diamond costs about 30-50 thousand. And the most expensive precious stone in the world is the red diamond: a carat is estimated at 500 thousand - 1 million dollars.

What Is the Difference Between Precious and Semi-Precious

There are no objective parameters that distinguish precious stones from semi-precious ones. The main criterion, in this case, is the price: semi-precious ones are inexpensive, and precious ones are not accessible to everyone. In the Research Institute of Jewelry Industry classification, the concept of precious and semi-precious stones is completely absent: they are jewelry, ornamental, and ornamental. Gems mined are highly rated on the world market. Moreover, in the Russian Federation, there are deposits of almost all precious minerals, except perhaps rubies. Classifying stones by properties In classifying precious stones, their various physical, optical, and other characteristics are considered. The most obvious characteristic of gemstones is their weight. Other things being equal, a carat of a large mineral will cost more than a similar unit of a small one (sometimes at times).

All other properties of gems can be combined into the following broad groups:

- Rarity.

The rarer the mineral, the higher it is valued.

A large enough deposit to empty - the stone immediately soars in price.

- Feeling.

Tactile sensations when touched ("soapy," slippery, and so on).

- Density.

The denser the stone, the heaviest it is. Zircon is even heavier than diamond. The lightest is amber.

- Hardness.

Here it is appropriate to mention the Mohs scale, which grades the hardness of substances according to a ten-point system, from diamond (10) and corundum (9) to talc. The test is scratching the surface.

- Strength.

A very hard stone may not be strong and easily crack under physical impact. Not too hard Jade is very difficult to split due to its high viscosity, and zircon crumbles instantly.

- Cleavage.

The description of this characteristic is rather complicated: it is the "behavior" of the stone when splitting (in what directions it splits). It is fundamentally important when cutting.

- Electrification and polarity.

For the jewelry industry, these parameters are not fundamental.

- Transparency.

Gemstones are usually transparent or translucent. The purer the gemstone, the more valuable it is.

- Color.

Multi-colored stones can be more valuable or cheaper than classic counterparts. Examples have been given above. Shine. It can be diamond, glass, silky, mother-of-pearl, etc. Light refraction. A characteristic that is fundamentally important when choosing a cut.

- Dichroism and polychroism.

A stone's ability to change color depends on the light's angle and intensity.

- Asterism.

The effect of the "star" inside the stone when hit by light.

- Luminescence.

The ability to glow is characteristic of diamonds, rubies, Jade, and other stones.

- Defectiveness.

The presence, location, type, and several various defects.

- Cut
  quality.

The value of the mineral directly depends on the quality of the cut.

- Refinement.

A stone with good natural characteristics will always cost more than an improved (heated, oiled, painted, etc.) counterpart.

Book 4
Rockhounding Locations

America is the second largest continent, with abundant mineral resources. It has minerals famous for their beauty and other beautifully colored semi-precious stones. Our collection of Minerals of America includes a beautiful representation of North and South America, with the most distinct origins of each mineral.

The specimens from various countries have been carefully selected (we only choose high-quality pieces), considering their crystalline system, color, and texture. They come presented in a full natural wood box with interchangeable boxes. Ideal as an educational gift for children and adults of all ages.

The Collection Includes 15 Representative Samples of the following Minerals:

Amethyst – Uruguay, Tourmaline – Brazil, Aventurine – Brazil, Quartz - United States, Lepidolite - United States, Barite – Argentina, Lapis Lazuli – Chile, Pyrite – Peru, Obsidian – Mexico, Fluorite – Argentina, Mica – Canada, Oligisto – Bolivia, Galena - United States, Calcite - the United States and Agate - Brazil.

The minerals are glued with hot silicone, and if desired, the silicone can be easily removed without damaging the piece with ethyl alcohol and thus separate them from the base where they are glued.

Locations To Find Gemstones in the USA

Gem digging can be lucrative, especially if you're a gem and mineral lover. Rock hunting and excavation sites are open in the United States at different times. Most digging sites consist of landfills from private mines, but sometimes private mining companies will let you dig digging sites on their land. Always contact the dig site owners ahead of time to know the current fees and equipment to bring with you to dig.

Northeast Places

Maine has the largest concentration of archaeological sites in the northeastern United States. Tourmaline, quartz, and rose quartz have been found at sites between Bethel and South Paris, mainly on Mount Mica. If you're in this area of Maine, look for Bethel Outdoor Adventures, Songo Pond Mine, West Maine Mineral Adventures, and West Paris Berchem. Hermit Island on the coast of The garnet mines of Green's Farm in Roxbury, Connecticut, have large dark red to black garnet crystals up to an inch wide. Staurolite crystals are also found here. At the Ruggles Mine in Grafton, New Hampshire, 150 gemstones can be found, among which the most common are amethyst, garnets, rose, and smoky quartz. Herkimer Diamonds is located at the Crystal Grove diamond mine in St. Johnsville, New York, in the Adirondack Mountains, which also hosts a family campsite.

Southeast Places

Franklin, North Carolina, is also called the "Gem of the World Capital." There are rubies and sapphires in the vicinity of the Columbia Mine and the Cowie Mountain Mine. The nearby Emerald Hollow Mine in Hiddith, North Carolina, is the only public emerald mine in the world. The Jackson Crossroads Amethyst Mine in Tignal, Georgia, is known for its deep purple amethyst. The Diamond Hill Quartz Mine in Antreville, South Carolina, has quartz and smoky quartz in various varieties. Occasionally, crystals of amethyst, pyrite, and calcite were found at this place.

Diamonds State Park in Murfreesboro, Arkansas, is the world's only publicly open diamond mining site. The best time to search for gems in the diamond field is after a rainstorm. The Arrowhead Crystal Mine offers two digging holes in the Ouachita Mountains in Mount Ida, Arkansas. Rubies, sapphires, tourmalines, and agates are found in pits at this site.

Northwest Places

Dig fire opals in the raw matrix at the Juniper Ridge Opal Mine between Klamath Falls and Lakeview, Oregon. Richardson Rock Ranch outside Madras, Oregon, has rocky ridges filled with thunderclouds and ledges of agate. Oregon Sunstone Hole Digging is available at the Spectrum Sunstone Public Mine near Plush, OR. In this area, large deposits of red and green sunstone lie in pits of volcanic rocks. Visit the Bentonite Mine in Coalinga, California, to find the California State Gem. Benitoite is a rare and valuable gemstone only harvested from the bentonite mine.

Southwest Places

Dig up quartz crystals, lepidolite, Topaz, morganite, and tourmalines at the Himalayan Tourmaline Mine excavation site in Santa Isabel, California. The Oceanview Mine is located in the famous Pala mining area in California. Here you can find a lot of tourmalines, kunzite, and aquamarine. Look for fire opals at the century-old Bonanza Opal Mine in Denio, Nevada. Utah has several free digging spots in state parks open to the public. Sunstone Claw in Millard County, Utah, has small sunstones scattered throughout the soil on the east side of the hill. Mount Topaz in Huab County, Utah, contains amber-colored topaz crystals and amethyst, garnet, opal, and hematite in the mountain's rhyolite deposits. Dig in Blanchard at the Desert Rose Mine in the Hansonburg mountain region for rare gems in the southwest. This site is located in Bingham, New Mexico, and the Blanchards also offer guided tours throughout the area. More than 80 different minerals have been collected at this site, including fluorite, barite, galena, linarite, and wulfenite. Rockhound State Park is also located in New Mexico outside of Demming. Dig all over the West

Popular Gem Hunting Locations in The United States

When you think of mining the "big four" gemstones (diamonds, rubies, sapphires, and emeralds), it's not hard to imagine places like

India, South Africa, and Colombia. However, you can find these and many other gems at gem hunting locations in the United States. Most of these places don't have the economic scale of mines in other countries but offer exciting gemology-themed getaways for the solo seeker and the whole family.

Pack up your gear and head to one of these famous American destinations. You can find thousands of dollars worth of gems in places where treasures you never imagined can be found.

Hiddenite Emerald Hollow Mine, North Carolina

Find beautiful, brilliant emeralds at Hiddenite, about an hour's drive from Winston-Salem, North Carolina. This Hollow Emerald Mine is home to the only emerald mine in the United States opens for public treasure hunting. You can view mine discoveries at the locks or do your prospecting, digging, and hunting for a small fee.

Although known primarily for emeralds, the 70-acre site also produces sapphires, tourmalines, garnets, topazes, and aquamarines. (The town of Hiddenite was named for the gemstone hiddenite, a rare variety of spodumene found in the area.) Open all year round, and the mine also has beautiful scenery.

Coordinates: 35.913786805192466, -81.08285500236073

Murfreesboro Diamond Crater State Park, Arkansas

Do you want to mine diamonds? Murfreesboro is the place to be. This Diamond Crater State Park, Located 120 miles from Little Rock, AR, is the only mine where visitors can search for diamonds and preserve their discoveries. Stay at the park campsite and enjoy the wildlife and nature along with some sparkling stones.

Coordinates: 34.032580310821196, -93.6729416071504

Gem Mountain, Spruce Pines, North Carolina

Looking for aquamarine? Go to Spruce Pine's house Gem Mountain. The Blue Ridge Mountains are perfect for finding beautiful blue stones, rubies, and moonstones. An on-site gemologist can examine his finds to see if they are genuine, while a gem artisan can modify and turn your gemstones into jewelry before you go home.

Coordinates: 35.87275132434118, -82.05020750236199

Cherokee Ruby and Sapphire Mine in Franklin, North Carolina

Search for rubies within Cherokee Ruby and Sapphire Mine. You can sift through rocks and dirt to find precious treasures, such as sapphires, garnets, and rutile.

The ticket price is low, the fun is great, and it's suitable for the whole family. The public is allowed for gem hunting from April to October. With the stunning background of the Blue Ridge Mountains, it will be a beautiful summer vacation.

Coordinates 35.27295418994107, -83.35128693121533

Gem Mountain Sapphire Mine, Philipsburg, Montana

Montana is without any doubt one of the most beautiful states in the country and a great destination for finding gems. Check Gem Mountain Sapphire Mine Go on a stellar exploration. What do you find when you examine the dirt and gravel at Gem Mountain? Sapphire – and many more.

The staff will help you clean and assess your gems, letting you know which ones are worth saving and potentially turning into wearable items.

Coordinates: 46.24747733492034, -113.5919589173641

Morefield Mine in Amelia, Virginia

The Morefield mine, less than an hour's drive from Richmond, Virginia, is known for its large amount of amazonite. Prospecting here can reward you with garnet, amethyst, beryl, Topaz, and many other minerals.

Seekers can use drainage techniques or collect from mines. The Morefield Mine has its stone exhibit on the site and one at the Smithsonian Institution in Washington, D.C.

Coordinates: 37.35841520283953, -77.91859073115343

More Gem Hunting Locations Open to The Public
Stellar meteorites can form a natural cross, inspiring countless legends. You can pick up these so-called "fairy stones" or "fairy crosses" on the ground. Scien Rock State Park in Stewart, Virginia.

Gem Quest Alternatives
Looking for a gem-themed vacation but don't want to get outdoors? There are many gems shows in the U.S. where you can look for gems indoors (or in the shade).

Every February, the Tucson, Arizona Gem, and Mineral Show attracts visitors from around the world.

Coordinates: 32.203851908021306, -110.98037616183214

Costa Rica
Enjoying the landscapes and natural trails offered by the Turrubares River while observing, collecting, and learning about the semi-precious stones that are located along the river is part of the attraction offered by the Rutas de Montañas Costa Rica group, which promotes rural tourism, always respecting nature and creating awareness among the participants.

Miguel Carmona, a baquiano who knows the area, uses the Costa Rican Scout Guides method to explore the areas and at the same time generate a positive impact, cleaning the garbage from the rivers while walking along the nature trails.

"One walks along the trails, near the river, if we see any stone, we select it, classify it, take photos of it and then return it so as not to kill the ecosystem; the idea is to track it down and find out where it comes from and analyze the currents and others," Carmona said.

Although mining in the country is illegal, as long as it is environmentally sustainable, it is possible, according to the authorities.

"Mining is prohibited; that's why we locate and describe them; they can't be taken, much less go to sell them. We don't mess with large stones that can serve as a den for animals in the river," added the naturist.

The available walks are for all ages and have a low level of difficulty; the stones are crossed to cross from the side, but these are not high, nor do they threaten the integrity of the hikers.

The route consists of 5 kilometers, a round trip from the base where the minibusses arrive.

Along the way, you could find stones such as turquoise, jasper, agate, and quartz.

During the tour, you can also visit jets of crystal clear waters, springs and small waterfalls, and rivers with thermal waters.

This hike takes place on the Turrubares River, near the area's breaker.

Weather conditions could vary schedules due to the possibility of headwaters from heavy rains in the mountains.

As a recommendation, they ask people to wear comfortable or long pants, and the shoes must be tennis or rubber for the wet journey and save that. Also, bring enough water, a cold lunch or snack, a bathing suit, moisturizer, sunscreen, lipstick, a hat, a cap, sunglasses, and extra clothes and shoes.

Coordinates: 9.865811632466158, -84.51309356620166

North Carolina

Diamond. The hardest known mineral is hardly found in western North Carolina. Thirteen diamonds have been reported from this region since 1843 from a 1.33-carat octahedral crystal from Brindletown Creek Ford in Burke County.

Likewise, does black sand mean Gold? Black sands (mostly iron sands) can be, and usually are, an indicator of Gold, but not always. The rule of thumb is that you usually find black sand with Gold, but not always gold with black sand. However, it's worth trying to see what happens if you find Gold and get black sands.

Are there opals in North Carolina? Opal mines in North Carolina | Walker Creek Kyanite, Buncombe County, North Carolina, pegmatite region.

Also, where are rubies mined in North Carolina?

Rubies are mostly found at Coey Creek, north of Franklin in Macon County. The rubies were also sourced from the Grimshaw Mine near Montvale in Jackson County. Ruby and pink corundum gemstones were recovered from the mines at Buck Creek in Clay County.

Where To Find Emeralds In North Carolina?

Where is the Gold in the river? Gold will accumulate at the head or foot of a stream bed or at bends in streams where the current slows or the slope of the channel decreases. Deposition sites can be pockets behind boulders, obstructions, and even mossy coastal areas.

Can you find Gold in any stream? Yes, Gold can be in rivers and streams, although not the Gold we see in the movies. Instead of the typical large gold nuggets, Gold in streams is usually found in tiny amounts, such as flakes or grains. They are called "placer gold."

Can you check Gold with a magnet? Yes, you can test Gold and silver with a magnet to determine if each material will be attracted to a magnetic force. Since both metals don't have to be magnetic, you'll be able to tell if they're counterfeit based on how they react to a magnet.

City	Stones and minerals	Coordinates
Brasstown, area north of Highway 64	Pomegranate	35.15259906233076, -92.56644483128153
Shooting Creek, outcrops, and gravel	Geodes (hyalite opal geodes)	35.89106762422289, -93.44037160057192

Where TO FIND GEODES IN North Carolina?
Are NC Rubies Valuable?
Rubies are already rarer than diamonds. But star rubies are something incredibly special. A collection of four "extraordinary" rare star rubies discovered outside of Asheville, North Carolina, almost 30 years ago. It could be worth more than $90 million - ended up at an auction house in New York.

Can You Find Gems in The Creeks Of North Carolina?
The Emerald Hollow Mine in North Carolina allows visitors to hunt for more than 60 natural gems and minerals, including emeralds, sapphires, and quartz. To search for gems, visitors can engage in

sluice (using the flow of water to search for gems), crawl (sorting mud in search of gems) or dig.

Coordinates: 35.91383894091376, -81.08284427352484

What Is the Nickname N.C.?

They called themselves " tar heels " as an expression of national pride. Others adopted the term, and North Carolina became commonly known as the "Tar Heel State." In the 1880s, as UNC teams began competing in intercollegiate sports, they needed a nickname.

Is There Gold in Every River?

Gold exists in extremely dilute concentrations in freshwater and seawater and is technically present in all rivers.

What soil is Gold found in? Soils are associated with gold deposits. The best-known type of soil that indicates Gold's presence is " black sand. " Black sands, of course, are not evidence of the presence of Gold nearby, but only that there are many minerals and heavy metals in the soil, one of which is Gold.

Doc's Rocks Gem Mine, Blowing Rock, North Carolina
Coordinates: 36.14176155650601, -81.66920011584635

Montana

In the interior of the limestone mountains, large caves, abysses, and galleries are discovered that keep something more than beautiful shapes in the dark.

Rainwater and meltwater infiltrate the limestone massifs and begin their underground journey. It circulates through the fractures of these soluble rocks, generating a network of ducts that end up converging, and finally, the water goes outside, causing springs or fountains.

But this trip gives for much more! On its way through the interior, the water transports chemical compounds in solution and drags rock particles of different sizes. When the energy of the water drops, it leaves its load, filling the cavities with sediments: silt, sand, gravel. Slowly circulating water also leaves its load in the solution when conditions are right.

Minerals precipitate from the water, creating rock deposits inside the cavities. These forms are called speleothems (from the Greek spelaion, cave, and theme, deposit) and have very different shapes depending mainly on the surface on which they grow and different names according to their shape: stalactites that hang from the ceiling, stalagmites that grow from the ground, columns when both are joined, pavements and gours in floors and ramps, castings on walls, curtains on sloping ceilings, pearls wrapping small fragments or nuclei.

They are beautiful forms; they often delight us and leave us in awe of this beautiful, slow work of water. But let's not just be mesmerized by their beauty; we have to look further to see that these speleothems keep a great secret. And it is that the sign of the past's climate is registered in them. Its formation depends on what happens on the surface since the active events in the cave respond to the events that occur outside, above the cavity.

A speleothem is an ancient file, a record of the external climate that must be deciphered and for which it requires the experience and work of the geologist. You must first choose the one that is of interest for your study, and stalagmites are normally used because they have a more continuous record, and then analyze their composition and date it.

Throughout the Quaternary (in the last 2.5 million years), there have been periods of cold and warm weather with very different rainfall and temperatures. The study of the stalagmites in the caves gives us a good understanding of how the climate has changed in the Pyrenees. Today all this is very important to us to assess what we are facing in the context of global change.

Gem Mountain Sapphire Mine, Philipsburg, Montana
Coordinates: 46.24756636850351, -113.59191600202054

Spokane Bar Sapphire Mine, Helena, Montana
Coordinates: 46.66482658721044, -111.81140890200543

Places To Dig for Rocks and Gems In California

California is an affordable place to find gemstones, with a wide variety. Many people like to go digging for them while they are in California. San Diego is even known as one of the largest producers of gemstones.

The best spots are usually in mines that are open to the public, specifically in the Pala mining district. There are also some free options, but they risk finding less precious stones, and no equipment is provided.

This book is for you if California rockhounding is next on your adventure list. Read on for the nine best places to hunt for gems in California.

Himalayan Mine
The Himalayan Mine is an accessible place for the public to visit to find precious stones. They are located at Lake Henshaw Resort, where you will be allowed to dig a screen through the mud from the mine.

Coordinates: 33.2350496939188, -116.76337718709347

What Gemstones to Expect

Many people go on digs hoping to find a certain type of crystal, so you will need to know what types of stones or gemstones pop up in different minds. The Himalaya mine often produces a wide variety of gemstones:

- A variety of tourmaline
- Quartz
- Clevelandite
- Spessartine
- Garnet
- lepidolite

Plumas County Gold Panning

Plumas County is in Northern California and has been known for panning for Gold since the 1800s. Most of these camps have since been torn down, but there are still several areas where the public can pan for any gold they find.

Coordinates: 39.93132738433511, -120.81338191866774

Price To Dig

Gold seine in these areas is generally free to the public. You can pan for Gold in any area that has not been staked. There are also public areas where inexperienced prospectors prefer to go.

The Caribou Gold Mining Association offers gold panning lessons and equipment. You'd have to visit them while you're in town or message them on Facebook to find out more about them.

Gemstones In Shasta County, California

Instructions:

- Visit Redding, California, and then start to make your way approximately 10 miles east on Hwy. 299 towards the town of old Shasta. The area of old Shasta is famous for being one of the richest areas in Gold during the 1900s, and prospectors still get lucky there from time to time.

Coordinates: 40.599297056459434, -122.4918045887229

Visit the main Museum at Old Shasta State Park and talk to the park rangers. Sale of maps and are happy to advise. The Museum also sells metal and plastic gold containers and nuggets if you can't find your own and need someone to impress.

- 10 miles east of French Gulch, California, visit the historic French Gulch Hotel. The owners provide maps, equipment, and advice to treasure hunters.

Coordinates: 40.69965939418987, -122.63881984083784

Wander into the unmarked bar street to hear old grizzly prospectors chat about hot spots. Some are for rent, and they will gladly show you the old mines, creeks, and lake beds, which you would not otherwise find in the foothills.

- Arrive at a destination with or without a guide and be willing to get dirty. Wear rubber boots if you plan to use a gold pan to sift through creek bottoms, and wear safety goggles if you plan to chip into rock walls.

Camas Creek will often produce agates and quartz pieces; you may even find a sliver or nugget of Gold if you're lucky. Rock walls often produce quartz veins that can be carefully hammered to expose gold and copper shards.

Look for clear and white quartz. It is rare and precious in Shasta County and makes beautiful decorative items and garden supplies.

Tips And Warnings

- Do not go to private property. Respect the Earth and fix the damage it causes. Leave the land as it seemed to you.

Opal In California?
Where Is Opal Hill?

Opal Hill, in eastern California near the Arizona border, is famous for its beautiful opal eggs, quartz crystals, and wonderful fire agates. Sometimes called Coon Hollow, this site is located deep in the Mule Mountains, not far from Palo Verde, CA.

Coordinates: 33.52297284435925, -114.86809704732565

Crystals In California?

- Himalaya Mine, Mesa Grande District, California.

  - **Coordinates:** **33.214501860624694, -116.80038696926933**

- Gold Prospecting Adventures, Jamestown, California.

  - **Coordinates:** **37.96103963958226, -120.41864780229912**

- The OceanView Mine, San Diego County, California.

  - **Coordinates:** **33.3861395981209, -117.04567238894046**

Where Can I Find Gemstones in Northern California?

The best places to rockhound in Northern California include locations near the cities of Crescent City and Eureka, as well as Siskiyou, Trinity, Modoc, and Mendocino counties.

Where can I find rocks in Southern California?

- Afton Canyon

    - **Coordinates:** **35.024903936794885, -116.35654795434314**

- Wiley's Well

    - **Coordinates:** **33.49445202569389, -114.88990111517604**

- Palo Verde Mountains

    - **Coordinates:** **33.351939327073914, -114.82902299989593**

- Mountain Chief

    - **Coordinates:** **48.840689431085174, -99.74702892857594**

- Clear Creek

- ○ **Coordinates:** **39.735960598244624, -105.69455297289466**

- Calico Mountains.

  - ○ **Coordinates:** **35.12477290981334, -116.90933282136737**

Where Can You Find Geodes in California?

Riverside and Imperial Counties have the best concentration of geode sites in Southern California.

Coordinates: 33.39263383226438, -114.9796484289148

- How can you tell if an opal is raw?

The variety of natural opal is determined by the body tone and transparency characteristics. Body Tone: The base tones of light, dark, and black opal range from colorless white through various shades of gray to black. Transparency: Opal of any body color will be opaque, translucent, or transparent.

- Can you find black opal in California?

The Western Trail from California to Washington supplies black opal, fire opal, and common opal varieties.

- Can diamonds be found in California?

The diamonds found in California are still something of a mystery. Its occurrences are unlike most other diamond deposits found around the world. Instead of being found within a hard rock source, all diamonds come from alluvial placer deposits.

- Can you find crystals in California?

Opal Hill Mine, Mule Mountains District, Riverside County, California. Opal Hill, in eastern California near the Arizona border, is known for its beautiful opal eggs, quartz crystals, and wonderful fire agates, making it one of the best places to look for gems in California.

Coordinates: 33.45351834824023, -114.86628864681711

- Can you find jade in California?

It is often found in California's riverbeds and outcrops of older rock formations.

- Where can I find Yooperlites in California?

These sparkling stones can be found on the shores of Lake Superior. Beaches near the Grand Marais area, Keweenaw Peninsula, and Whitefish Point are great for looking for Yooperlights.

Coordinates: 47.81488571493412, -86.95932832782375

- Can you find agates in California?

Agate (ag·it) is abundant throughout Southern California and comes in various colors and patterns. It usually forms within volcanic and metamorphic rocks and consists mainly of chalcedony and quartz.

Amethyst in California?

The Purple Heart Mine is in the Kingston Range of San Bernardino County in Southern California.

Coordinates: 32.7987328807994, -108.57898085946907

- Where can I get a black fire opal?

Virgin Valley in northern Nevada is the only place in North America where black fire opal is found in significant quantity.

Coordinates: 36.569869263330745, -114.33529565238108

- Is gem mining real?

The gems you find in the buckets you buy at the gem mine are rough gems that you can take home by polishing yourself with a piece of sandpaper while you watch T.V. or read, or you can pay for the gem that people polish and place on a piece of jewelry.

- What is the rarest opal color?

Black opal is the unique and most prized form of opal and has a black (or dark) body tone. Black opals come in all colors of the rainbow.

Utah

You can't match the thrill of finding and taking your gemstones. If you're a beginner, pick up a guide like "Gem Identification Made Easy" or "Collecting Stones, Gems, and Minerals: Identification Made Easy." You can also take a gemology class at your local community college or an area club. Finding semi-precious stones in Utah, where gemstones are abundant throughout much of the state, is just a matter of knowing where to look.

Instructions:

- The appearance of geodes at Dugway Geode Beds, near Vernon, Utah, in Juab County. Visitors have removed more major samples from the surface, but if you dig a little, you'll find a wide variety of geodes. The beds feature deep holes where you can jump into and dig for gems. Pay attention not to dig too deep into the walls of any pit, as dangerous cave-ins can occur.

Coordinates: 39.89424659981356, -113.1368422734022

- Spend a day at Topaz Mountain, also in Juab County, where you will find a wide variety of gemstones, such as Beryl, Garnet, Hematite, Calcite, Chalcedony, Amethyst, Fluorite, Cassiterite, Durangite, Bixbyite, Pseudobrucite and Topaz, a gemstone from the state of Utah. The Topaz here is naturally amber in color but becomes clear after exposure to light. These gems formed within the cavities of an area volcano that erupted 6 to 7 million years ago. You may have to look for Topaz crystals of excellent shape, size, and quality.

Coordinates: 39.70955394382646, -113.10330433547742

Visit the world-famous Wheeler's Amphitheater in Antelope Springs, 54 miles west of Delta, Utah. Here you can find gemstones (also known as yellow labradorite) and Aragonite. Fossils can also be found, although visitors are prohibited from extracting fossils from the rock face of the quarry.

Coordinates: 39.0905867511924, -114.2450836145861

- Search for agate, chert jasper---varieties of microcrystalline or cryptocrystalline quartz---as petrified wood near Capitol Reef National Park in Wayne County, one of the state's prime harassing rock areas. To get there, drive 8.5 miles west on Utah Highway 24, where the road crests. Along the north side of the road, you'll find agate, chert, jasper, petrified ancient black wood, and huge rocks. The chert and agate are white, green, grey, orange, purple, and red, jasper is usually red, and petrified wood is tan.

Coordinates: 38.31982405566177, -111.24016401817671

Gems In Utah?

A staggering 80 percent of Utah is allocated for public use, which offers outdoor gem-mining opportunities. The state contains crystals and minerals not found anywhere else. Many sites designated for the public allow individual collectors to extract and dispose of small amounts of gemstones.

- Sites near Milford, Utah

One of Utah's largest exposed plutonic bodies, or igneous rock masses, is found in Utah's Ore Mountains in Beaver County. Sites like Corral de la Roca Recreation Area contain pockets of clear smoky quartz crystals, obsidian, garnets, blue beryl, and much more. This public site is off Highway 21 in Milford, Utah, owned by the Bureau of Land Management.

Coordinates: 38.37745303623876, -112.83493320996556

- Sites near Lynndyl, Utah

In Juab County, at the southern end of the Thomas Range, Topaz Mountain attracts rock collectors searching for Utah's state gem, the Topaz. Although the semi-precious gemstone is found in various colors, most Topaz on this site is amber or transparent. Light Topaz is relatively easy to find in washes in the area. Searching for rock vegetation can cause spots containing pockets of the most sought after amber colored version. Topaz Mountain is an ideal place for beginners and experts alike. For true rock hounds, some off-the-beaten-path spots can be accessed by ATVs and often contain more gemstones than pick-up sites near the road. The mountain is located near Lynndyl, Utah,

Coordinates: 39.710148201810085, -113.10343308150807

- Sites near Cheney, Utah

The result of pockets of gas trapped in a cooling flow of lava, black, metallic, and purple amethyst Bixbyite crystals found in the Cheney region between Utah up to an inch long. A rarer find, the mineral rutile contains needle-like crystals, while Bixbyite occurs in isometric, cube-shaped forms. Breaking or prying open cracks in rhyolite, a dark gray white rock in the area reveals crystals. The site is located on Route 89 North.

Coordinates: 41.895728614214946, -111.46948750031456

- Utah Mining Tips

Depending on your dig location, the gems you're looking for, and other mining variables, the tools you need can range from picks to shovels, chisels, and sledgehammers. Safety glasses are always highly recommended to prevent flying and debris from injuring the eyes or face. In addition to mining tools, you should take plenty of water and a hat or other head covering due to extreme heat and sun exposure.

Nevada

Here are some areas where the public can go and dig:

- Bonanza opal mine.

    o **Coordinates:** **41.83394986672412,**
    -119.07759397928963

- Garnet Hill Recreation Area.

    o **Coordinates:** **39.2915075205233,**
    -114.94724664458555

- Kokopelli Opals.

  - **Coordinates:** **41.82077412525391, -119.07554054450314**

- Rainbow opals.

  - **Coordinates:** **41.795587760290886, -119.01502038683212**

- Royal Peacock Opal Mine.

  - **Coordinates:** **41.786149077119155, -119.1002645886838**

- Royston Turquoise Mine.

  - **Coordinates:** **40.167714168509946, -116.66369663524083**

- Anaconda Copper Mine (Nevada)

  - **Coordinates:** **38.98546237144038, -119.20518322931063**

- Where is turquoise found in Nevada?

Most of the Pilot Mountain District turquoise is found in vein form. Pilot Mountain: The Pilot Mountain mine is one of Nevada's most productive turquoise mines.

Coordinates: 36.34058697490798, -80.47439589852148

- What kind of rocks are in Nevada?

Nevada has a wide variety of rocks and minerals. Igneous rocks include gabbro, diorite, granite intrusions, flows, breccia, and tuffs of basalt, andesite, and rhyolite. Sedimentary rocks include conglomerate, sandstone, siltstone, slate, argillite, limestone, and dolomite.

Where Can I Go Rock Hunting in Arizona?

Where to Go Rockhounding in Arizona (5 Best Rock Collecting Sites)

- Safford, AZ - Fire Agate.

    - **Coordinates: 32.865184427685506, -109.39633240244714**

- Payson, AZ - Crystals at Diamond Point.

    - **Coordinates: 34.29937162575074, -111.2045456893576**

- Woodruff, AZ - Petrified Wood.

    - **Coordinates: 34.9163711301603, -110.1581135715741**

- Wickenburg, AZ - Burro Creek Rockhounding Site.

    - **Coordinates: 34.53816989704036, -113.44992770240053**

- Payson, AZ - Fossils at Indian Gardens Paleo Site.

  - **Coordinates:** **34.3223451662786, -111.1110220600785**

- Where is Gold mined in Nevada?

Where Can You Rockhound in Nevada?

Fortunately, you can: There are three rock hound locations in Nevada, and most of them will open for the season this spring.

- Garnet Hill in Ely.

  - **Coordinates:** **39.291499217111074, -114.94733247527265**

- Royston Turquoise Mine in Tonopah.

  - **Coordinates:** **38.50117678858176, -117.55844820018766**

- Opal mines near Denio.

  - **Coordinates:** **41.88553230434275, -118.9977335937818**

Where Can I Find Black Opals in Nevada?

In the Sheldon National Wildlife Refuge near Denio in northwestern Nevada, Virgin Valley is home to the finest opal deposits that produce the world's brightest Black, Crystal, Fire, and other opal types.

Coordinates: 41.818889777071796, -119.23249611725159

- Where can I find quartz in Nevada?

Quartz And Amethyst

The stone can be obtained at a mountain junction known as Hallelujah Junction. Cute Quartz Crystals can be found everywhere. Nevada. They are commonly found by metal detectorists looking for Gold and meteorites in northern Nevada. Clear and smoked varieties are found throughout the state.

Coordinates: 39.775180937242816, -120.03870256613074

- Are diamonds found in Nevada?

Some people did notice the variety of metals in Nevada, though, and some strikes were made in lead, manganese, nickel, and marble. There was even a platinum mine, but no one expected to find diamonds.

- What is the jewel of the state of Nevada?

Considered one of Nevada's most beautiful gemstones, Virgin Valley Black fire opal was designated a precious gemstone on May 27, 1987.

Coordinates: 36.57852077506411, -114.41894094931533

International Rockhounding

Ontario has several hotspots for recreational geology. These places might allow you to discover a new rock or mineral specimen on your bucket list, and they can allow you to learn about Ontario's past.

Bancroft

The area surrounding the township in Hastings County is famous for amateur geology. The area, which is part of the Canadian Shield, is between 1.1 and 1.8 billion years old. Mining activities began at the end of the 19th century, but the veins found were small. Unlike other parts of the province, the mines temporarily closed until the uranium boom of the late 1950s, when three mines reopened. However, the veins found were small, and industrial mining activities ceased, given the high costs. But the region has become a geology enthusiast's paradise due to the pyrite, mica, apatite, rose quartz, and white quartz. Bancroft has been dubbed the mining capital of Canada.

Coordinates: 44.496921085324736, -77.65829175069744

- Miner's Loop is a good start is following this automobile route, which encompasses Millside Park

  - **Coordinates: 42.3030448013341, -72.66312662545121**

- the Deloro Mine Site

  - **Coordinates: 44.51024979119285, -77.62094157509797**

- the Marmoraton Mine Site.

  - **Coordinates: 44.497845652146765, -77.65440310820523**

Richardson Mine

Another popular location for amateur geology is Ontario's first gold mine which sparked a gold rush that resulted in the opening of the Deloro, Gilmour, Cordova, Feigle, Bannockburn, and Golden Fleece mines.

Coordinates: 49.7755276395181, -86.99698004637123

Bonnechere Museum and Geoheritage Trail

Recognized as Canada's Ordovician Fossil Capital, this living Museum explores natural history along the Bonnechere River and offers guided tours and fossil searches.

Coordinates: 45.540749066096915, -77.10020684622553

Lakeside Gems

Stock up on all the geology tools you'll need and admire an impressive collection of minerals and semi-precious stones of local and international origin.

Coordinates: 45.02700112205976, -77.90428993275152

Eagles' Nest Lookout

This lookout perched atop a 200-foot rock offers a great view of Bancroft Township in the landscape below you.

Coordinates: 43.95799509545094, -93.48561148437743

Bancroft Rockhound Gemboree

July 28-31, 2022, was the Bancroft Rockhound Gemboree event, attended by over 100 dealers worldwide to display their gemstone specimens, minerals, and other treasures at the North Hastings Community Center and Curling Club Bancroft. You can also enjoy excursions, demonstrations, and workshops.

Coordinates: 45.0270996991103, -77.90417191555676

Sudbury

Almost two billion years ago, a huge meteorite created the second largest impact crater on Earth, resulting in rich nickel and copper ore deposits. The crater is 62 kilometers long, 30 kilometers wide, and 15 kilometers deep! This place is called the Sudbury Basin, where the largest concentration of mines in the world is located. By 1910, the Sudbury region produced 80% of the world's nickel. The center of Greater Sudbury lies to the south of what remains of the crater.

Coordinates: 46.54054174175138, -80.99554553145575

Kirkland Lake Mining Heritage Tour
Learn about Kirkland Lake's mining history along the "golden mile," a series of seven major mines.

Coordinates: 48.15963496737355, -80.01825164543563

Jane Goodall Rehabilitation Trail
In the years after the glory days of mining, the City of Greater Sudbury undertook the ecological restoration of many of the mining-damaged landscapes as part of a greening program. The Jane Goodall Rehabilitation Trail offers a self-guided tour of a rehabilitation and recovery site.

Coordinates: 46.49514198694096, -80.84116211707524

Cobalt Mining Museum
See the largest silver exhibit at the Cobalt Mining Museum.

Coordinates: 47.39568133148031, -79.68589751547096

Silver Heritage Trail
Established by the Cobalt Heritage Society, this self-guided tour takes you to various silver mines and mills in the Cobalt region.

Coordinates: 47.39250067326611, -79.6836075712344

Copper Cliff
Smelter Smokestack Take a GeoTour for a close-up view of this massive smokestack from a park in a nearby Copper Cliff Historic District and an overview of the early years of mining in the area.

Coordinates: 42.89306222301018, -90.32129307804077

Temiskaming Shores

Visit the distinctive and unusual landscapes of the "Little Clay Belt" in New Liskeard and Haileybury Townships, and learn about its unique geology.

Coordinates: 47.533294724445874, -79.6760500576564

Killarney

The town of Killarney stands on the rocky shores of Georgian Bay. Visit the surrounding landscapes of white mountains, crystal clear waters, and pink granite rocks that light up at sunset and sunrise, and learn about the area's geological origins.

Coordinates: 52.06017790255301, -9.508050074525334

French River Provincial

Park Located between Parry Sound and the city of Greater Sudbury, this park's visitor center showcases this famous waterway's history, geology, and ecology. Trails and a suspension bridge offer stunning views across the gorge to the rocky walls of the river.

Coordinates: 46.01723078583548, -80.58566093271607

Timmins

One of the richest gold deposits worldwide, Timmins has produced more Gold than any other mining camp in Canada in the last century. This GeoTour highlights the "Big Three" gold mines (Hollinger, Dome, and McIntyre) and restored urban parks from former mining sites.

Coordinates: 48.40459751803361, -81.32691466188352

Gowganda and Matachewan

These rural communities in the Timiskaming district have several nearby abandoned silver mines and silver arsenide ores. Barite mines contain calcite, fluorite, pyrite, and some rare finds of copper in rock debris.

Coordinates: 47.65011470350982, -80.76675469214018

Algoma Region

- Explore the mining and geological history of Elliot Lake

    - **Coordinates:** **46.38603592397115, -82.65351984845285**

- The Bruce Mines

    - **Coordinates:** **46.300334099609216, -83.79346027118649**

- St. Joseph Island

    - **Coordinates:** **46.22800357720678, -83.97111218682878**

- And the shores of majestic Lake Superior.

    - **Coordinates:** **46.5567238790205, -84.57652266830513**

- Nuclear and Mining Museum
- This attraction, located at the Ranger's Heritage Center in the Elliot Lake Fire Tower, traces the area's mining history.

    - **Coordinates:** **46.3875984882204, -82.62048357503089**

Bruce Mines

In the summer, guided tours are offered at the Simpson Mine Shaft, which has been restored to demonstrate how copper was mined in the mid-1800s. This area is on the borders of the Canadian Shield and the Lower Great Lakes and offers many opportunities for searching for various minerals and rocks. Common minerals include chalcopyrite, azurite, jasper, uraninite, and calcite crystals. It is even said that there are traces of Gold in the old mine near Ophir.

Coordinates: 46.298228960615944, -83.78989829767193

Desbarats

In this area, puddingstone can be found on the shores of Lake Huron and rippled sandstone formations along Highway 17, west of Desbarats and Highway.

Coordinates: 638. 46.3447717434095, -83.92247894718076

San Jose

Island St. Joseph Island has many limestone deposits, where you'll find brachiopod and trilobite fossils.

Coordinates: 46.23552242355384, -83.96979975488117

Lake Superior Provincial Park

Famous for its raw beauty along the shoreline, this park offers a motorized ride along the shores of the world's largest freshwater lake, Lake Superior. Even colored sand is made up of grains from various rocks and minerals.

Coordinates: 48.03928770154952, -88.72935463285899

Upper Lake Region

This area is home to the largest amethyst deposit in all of Canada.

Coordinates: 48.31857639487832, -95.02789741658775

Amethyst Mine Overview

A local family has operated this mine just 60 kilometers east of Thunder Bay for over 35 years. Today, it is used in jewelry. Your adventure begins at a beautiful visitor center and continues to the collection and excavation area. Guided tours and historical panels share interesting information about mining in this area.

Diamond Willow Amethyst Mine

From May through October, visitors are invited to collect many different types of amethyst on tour at this family-owned and operated amethyst mine. An on-site gift shop lets you purchase beautiful and colorful amethyst specimens and other unique gifts.

Coordinates: 48.68709131636982, -88.66546786180479

Nipigon

Another excellent GeoTour highlights nine well-known places of geological interest that illustrate these unique geological and geographic features, such as high cliffs and distinctive red rocks.

Coordinates: 49.01807744991644, -88.25225943075385

Etiquette in Amateur Geology

The hobby of amateur geology in Ontario is a privilege, not a right. Amateur geologists have no legal right to collect or extract minerals on Crown land or land owned by an individual or company other than the collector.

You should always get permission to search privately owned places.

Limit the amount of what you dig to what you can carry unassisted, use only hand tools, and dig a site once a year. In Ontario, amateur geology collects and markets minerals, not sells them.

The U.K.

Sometimes, to visit a strange place, with unrepeatable characteristics and away from the great masses of tourists, you do not have to cross half the world and reach the most remote place on the planet, but simply travel a couple of hours from the most visited city in Europe.

The United Kingdom is undoubtedly full of places to visit: cosmopolitan London, the Neolithic formations of Stonehenge, the Roman baths of Bath, Edinburgh, etc. In terms of landscapes and natural sites, it is not far behind, although it must be recognized that the first names that come to mind are works created by man and not nature.

The curious thing is that in the southwest of England, just four hours from London, there is a place almost without equal in the world and little visited despite being the only natural asset declared a World Heritage Site on the entire island. It is the Jurassic Coast or Jurassic Coast.

In a 150-kilometer stretch between the English counties of East Devon and Dorset lie the remains of 185 million years of the history of the Earth, spanning the Triassic, Jurassic, and Cretaceous periods, which together make up the Mesozoic era.

In this stretch of coast, the cliffs, beaches, and rock formations (which are not lacking in the rest of the island) stand out. In these places, the specialized eyes (and the less so with a little help) will be able to see the different layers of the planet. But the amazing thing is that apart from this, the entire area is mined with fossils, ranging from plants and small mollusks to large reptiles and mammals. Even so, it is true that being a coastal area, marine species prevail since they are continually exposed to the constant erosion of the cliffs.

If we are short on time and want to play it safe, Charmouth is the best place. But also, if we have already made the trip to this place, it is worth subtracting at least two days of exploring the area.

Suppose you do not completely trust the words of the writer. In that case, it is worth adding that due to the particular characteristics provided by the geological longevity of the area and its fossils, in 2017, National Geographic was encouraged to include the Lyme Regis and Charmouth stretch of beach among the best 21 beaches in the world.

Book 5 It's Time to Go!

Rockhounding Trip

The planning stage is very important, as it determines the success of your expedition. Here are some tips that will help you in this task:

1) Discuss with other rockhounds first and determine good places for rockhounding.

2) Decide which areas (forests, mountains, valleys, etc.) you would like to visit on this expedition. Make sure these areas have plenty of quarries, and also make sure they don't overlap or interfere with each other.

3) Decide what equipment you want to take with you, then purchase it from the local shops. The shops that sell camping supplies should have all the necessary items.

4) Once you've made your preparations, get some advice about the best place to go rockhounding from someone who has already been on a similar expedition.

Tools and safety measures:

When it comes to rockhounding, the right tools are essential for collecting the best samples. Many items needed are common household items, but most require a trip to the local hardware store.

Buy The Appropriate Rock Collecting Tools

- Check around your house before you shop. Many necessary tools, such as a hammer, can be brought from home.

- Take a trip to the hardware store. You will most likely have a couple of hammers around the house, but you will need different sizes, such as a sled, a crack hammer, a bricklayer hammer, and a chisel.

- Purchase eye protection. Glasses are usually enough, but make sure they are shock resistant. It can also be found at the hardware store.

- Get a loupe with 10x magnification. Geologists use too many small magnifying crystals not seen by the naked eye.
- Grab a small pint of brightly colored paint. Experienced rockhounds paint the handles of their tools, which can otherwise easily become lost in vast forests, fields, or riverbeds.
- Go with geologists' picks. They use a 4-pound crack hammer, pick hoe, and an 8-pound sled. Popular brand names include Estwing and Craftsman Tools.
- Buy a good pair of leather or cloth gloves, but it is preferred to use leather gloves. Blisters and sharp rock shards can put a nasty damper on your rock collecting experience.

Maximize The Use of Each Tool

- Build muscle or bring another set of hands. Many tools become heavy after repeated use, so bring your friends who enjoy rockhounding and share the workload!
- Break the big rocks. Use an 8-pound sled to cut through solid stone.
- Make use of your crack hammer. It is ideal for breaking medium rock and driving chisels.
- Imitate the great! Use the geologist's hammer, which has a spike on one end, to knock the rocks apart or out of the ground.
- Search for fossils using a bricklayer hammer. This tool has a chisel on one end and can be used to split friable or brittle rocks such as sandstone, which often contains fossils.
- Hard-to-reach access points with long, skinny chisels. These tools are ideal for removing rock from the most hazardous locations. Better is a variety of sizes and lengths.

Tips and Warnings

- Get a toolbox to carry and organize your tools. This will also help you easily see if you have accidentally left something behind.
- Never use your rock-picking tools without eye protection. Loose particles can become airborne and can damage your eyesight.

Safety

You know what safety equipment is for rock collectors. You never know what is out there in the fields, so it's best to be prepared, but a first aid kit and some basic tools should be enough for most rockhounding trips.

- A pair of sturdy boots (preferably waterproof) will help prevent blisters; if you plan on hiking through deep snow, ensure your boots have good treads.
- Be sure to carry plenty of food and water - especially if you're going into the wilderness. Don't forget to pack lots of energy bars too!
- If you're planning any off-trail explorations, bring along several maps of the area and a compass or GPS.
- Bring a flashlight if you'll be exploring at night. It's also wise to carry a small crossbow on nighttime excursions. Crossbows are quiet weapons that can penetrate heavy clothing without injuring the wearer. They can also fire bolts up to 50 yards away.
- There's no substitute for common sense - don't try anything stupid!
- Check weather reports before heading out, and be prepared for sudden temperature changes.
- Pack warm clothes and rain gear, just in case.
- Dress lightly when packing for summer trips, but remember to take a light jacket with you even in the hottest months.
- Expect cold and icy conditions when traveling through mountainous regions during the winter.
- In an emergency, bring a cell phone and plenty of extra batteries.
- Remember to leave a word about your itinerary with someone responsible - the last thing you want is for them to worry while you're out having fun.
- If you're going on a rock-hounding trip, tell someone where you're headed and how long you expect to be gone.
- Always tell someone where you're going and when you plan on returning.

- Track the dates and times you head out, and let family members know where you're going.
- Scan the weather forecast before heading out, and dress appropriately for the season.
- The best way to avoid getting lost is to stay on marked trails.
- When exploring new areas, keep your eyes open for hidden dangers: cliffs, drop-offs, and other hazards.
- Before embarking on any expedition, it's always a good idea to familiarize yourself with local landmarks.
- Stay alert and watch your step when climbing steep terrain.
- Watch out for loose rocks and falling tree branches.
- Avoid carrying anything that could become tangled in the cables of overhead power lines.
- If you're working near a high-voltage electrical line, ensure there aren't any nearby power lines.

Essential Tools for the Trip

Rock Hammer

Known as a rock hammer or geological pick, this tool is a versatile device that can help geologists extract rock samples. The tool is shaped like a hammer with a handle at one end. The other end is put to a dual purpose. One side of the head resembles a normal hammer. This is used to split open rocks to get minerals inside. Across the head is tapered into a chisel. It is used for rocks with a larger chip surface. The rock hammer is designed to save rockhounds time by eliminating the need to change tools often. Rock hammers are made from different materials and in different sizes to tackle various rock types.

Auger

Rock samples do not always come from the surface of the earth. Samples are also taken from within the earth. To get these samples, rockhounds need to drill a hole. Hand varieties are used in ice fishing, and motorized varieties are used in commercial activities. The drill works by turning like a corkscrew. This brings the minerals and soil to the surface behind the rotating blades. This process is ideal for rock sampling as the auger brings the material to the surface. However, care is needed when using a motorized variety as machine oil and lubrication can mar rock samples.

Containers

An essential rock sampling tool is a suitable container for sample placement. Most commonly used are clear plastic bags. These come in various sizes, and the rock can be seen through the plastic for quick identification. However, rock samples must be transported and stored submerged in water. Submerging some rock samples in water will slow down the oxidation process. When stored in this way, the rock samples are placed in glass or plastic boxes, which are rubber-sealed to prevent evaporation and contamination from outside elements.

Ways to Create a Custom Map for Your Trip

There are many options for creating maps: from traditional desktop GIS software or a web application.

Cloud GIS applications are ideal professional GIS tools to analyze, edit and visualize data online without installing software. However, using these tools requires learning, and their options can be overwhelming.

But there is good news. If we want to create custom maps, using an application with GIS capabilities is not necessary. In this book, we will see some simple alternatives that allow us to create our maps in a matter of seconds and, in many cases, without prior registration.

1. Mappin

Mappin allows you to create and download personalized maps, with payment options if you want a more elaborate document, easily with only five steps:

- Select the location.
- Add a pin.
- Select a style (the most elaborate ones cost between 2 and 3 dollars).
- Choose the design.
- Pick a border.

2. EZ MAP

EZ Map is advertised as a tool to create maps from Google Maps and embed them on our website. This tool removes the trauma of fighting Google Maps.

EZ Map allows us to select a region of the map that we want to embed in our web page and add different markers or controls on the web map. But the interesting thing about this tool is the possibility of using a wide variety of available themes based on Snazzy Maps. To save our maps, we must register.

3. GMAPGIS

GmapGIS is a simple tool that uses Google maps but without registration.

We can draw lines, and shapes, add labels and markers, and measure the distance on the map.

We can also add GeoJSON, KML files, or Google Fusion tables.

Once we have finished composing the map, a link is automatically generated that we can share. We can also choose if we want to save the map in a KML format or see it on Google Earth.

4. MAP CHART

Map chart allows us to create custom maps of the world, Europe, America, Africa, the United States, or the United Kingdom with colors and descriptions of our choice.

Map chart offers a custom color scheme from a selection of friendly color palettes.

The generated map is a high-resolution PNG image, which can be used and embedded on a website for free.

5. MAPINSECONDS.COM

MapInSeconds is a tool with which we can convert data from a spreadsheet into maps.

Its use is very intuitive. Simply copy the data from our Excel sheet and paste it into the application.

As in the previous tool, we can choose the color palette to customize the result further.

Once pasted, a map is automatically created that we can download in PPTX or PNG format.

In addition, since it does not require registration, composing a map is a matter of seconds.

Eye! We must have a column with the names of the regions (country, city, or province). Its operation is simple, but sometimes it does not read the regions well; it requires a little skill.

6. PIXELMAP GENERATOR

PixelMap Generator is a fantastic tool for creating custom pixel maps.

7. MAPHUB

MapHub stands out for its modern interface and allows us to create custom maps by choosing 20 base maps and adding markers, lines, polygons, or labels.

We can import and export data in the following formats:

- GeoJSON.
- KML/KMZ.
- GPX.
- Shapefile ZIP.
- JPG and PNG images.
- IGC.

Each map is assigned a URL that allows us to share on social networks or by email. To save the map, we need to register. It is highly Recommended! We see a lot of future for this tool.

8. Scribble Maps

Scribble Maps is a mapping tool that offers a convenient platform for drawing and sharing maps.

We can easily add custom images, place text and markers, draw shapes, calculate distances, save a map as a PDF, and much more.

We can also send maps to our friends or embed them on a website. The basic Scribble service is free, while Scribble Maps VIP (paid) allows us to import KML files, spreadsheets, and SHP files.

9. ZEEMAPS

ZeeMaps (We map your lists) allows us to design and publish interactive maps without prior registration.

We can create maps from data from Location (Search), Google spreadsheets, Microsoft Excel, CSV, KML, GeoRSS feed, or by Copy and Paste.

By using ZeeMaps, we can place customizable markers, highlight countries, states, and cities add video, audio, or sound clips, add customizable search fields to your map, create heat maps, make private maps, GeoSearch (search that meets a criterion of the value of a field and proximity), plan trips. And finally, export the map in PNG or PDF format and share the map (URL).

10. INFOGRAM

Infogram is a visual communication tool that allows anyone to easily create different types of interactive infographics, maps, social media images, and reports. Create amazing charts, maps, and dashboards in no time with Infogram.

You're ready! Now off to the woods.

After weeks of preparation, it's time to head into the wilderness with your friends. You can see that your clothes and gear are in good condition; all your purchases were from well-known stores specializing in outdoor products.

Your car is parked near the woods, but you decide not to use it today. It's better if you walk.

You notice several paths leading northward through the trees as you approach the forest. These paths look pretty easy to follow.

You step onto one path and begin walking northward. After an hour, you reach a clearing. The ground here is covered by pine needles, fallen branches, and pieces of wood. There are small rocks scattered across the area. This is your time to look for stones, so use your equipment wisely and take safety precautions. Then pick up a couple of them and start saving them in your containers or bags using the knowledge provided above.

It is the choice of a rockhound for how long he will search the field. But, after finding what you are looking for, it is time to fill your bags, pack up and return home.

Once you're on the road again, you think about what you might do differently next time you go rockhounding. For instance, wearing sturdy boots instead of sandals would probably be a good idea. And maybe it would be a great idea to bring some sandwiches and fruit, too.

There's nothing wrong with having goals, but it's important to keep these in perspective. You needn't always accomplish everything to feel successful. Once in a while, you have to sit back, relax and enjoy the wonderful experience this adventurous rockhounding trip brought you.

After The Trip

Back home, you unpack the rocks you found while rockhounding and place them carefully inside your bag. Then you put away all your camping gear. Your clothes are probably still damp from the rain or filled with dirt from the fields, but that's okay.

You retrieve your backpack from the corner of your room, where you left it after returning from your last rockhounding expedition.

You're happy to see it again; your latest rockhounding expedition was a great success, and you have many new specimens to show your friends.

You open up your backpack and remove the rocks.

Understand The Regulations and Risks of Mineral Exploration

Once you have thoroughly finished researching all the information to go hunting, you tell yourself that you are ready to start an adventure. Well, no! There are some little things to learn.

You should know first that removing stones from certain places may be prohibited. Therefore, we must include information regarding rules and safety in this article before we start prospecting and collecting minerals.

Learn About Mineral Extraction and Environmental Protection Laws

Because rocks and minerals can be valuable, regulations protect the people who own the mineral and those who own the area where the mineral may be.

Every place belongs to someone. You just have to ensure you have written permission giving you the right to walk around and collect certain minerals where you want to do it. Although hunting for minerals is a hobby like gold panning, it essentially responds to compliance with the mining code. Prospecting is, therefore, possible, subject to authorization.

This authorization must be made to the owner of private land, the prefecture, or the mining management service on public land.

Even if you have permission from the owner to go stone hunting, the owner may not be able to offer you this permission if he does not own the mineral rights. For more information, contact the associations near you.

Learn The Fundamentals of Mineral Hunting Safety

Rock prospecting is great fun and generally safe for people of all ages. However, nature comes with risks, just like any other outdoor activity. Most basic outdoor safety guidelines are common sense. You will have a great time if you have a good first aid kit if you never go prospecting alone and if you are alert to any weather hazards.

You will avoid problems by knowing the rules and how to be safe when prospecting for stones. Once you are familiar with the regulations in your area, know how to keep yourself safe, and know where you want to prospect for the stones, you are ready for the next phase: looking for them!

Start Prospecting for Stones and Minerals

You can get rocks for your collection in two ways: go out and search for them or buy them. Luckily, no matter where you live, getting rocks is pretty straightforward if you don't have a high budget and can find them anywhere. You can start right in your garden or near your home.

While the rocks in your garden may not be very valuable or fascinating, this is a great way to start learning to recognize the different rocks you come across. Limestone is not a collector's item, but knowing how to recognize it is very valuable.

It is a very pleasant pastime to practice with children and family members. They are already close to the ground and able to discover fascinating things!

You can learn a lot about where these types of rocks are found naturally if you explore the types of rocks you want to acquire. You can save a lot of time researching topographic and geological maps and determining where to look.

If you love to travel, collecting stones is one of those wonderful hobbies that can take you anywhere on this planet if you like it. You can plan a vacation to Brazil to look for agates or visit several gemstone mines that offer public tours. Maybe you'll even travel to Arkansas to search for gems in Diamond Crater State Park!

One of the common and preferred places is along streams, rivers, and streams since the waterways drain many minerals of all kinds that erode during floods.

The Etiquettes of Rockhounding

The Etiquette of Rockhounding involves respecting other people's property while digging for minerals. You need to follow certain rules when rockhounding, not to breach the ethical code of conduct for rockhounding. For example, it would be bad manners to dig around in someone else's yard without asking permission first. Also, you should never dig near a historical site or a cemetery. Some areas prohibit the removal of rocks from public lands, even if they aren't yours. These areas include national parks, state forests, wildlife refuges, and many city parks. It is also considered rude to disturb archaeological sites or burial grounds. Finally, you should leave the site just as you found it, leaving only the removed rocks.

Ancient Indian Tradition

Ancient Indians believed that the earth was alive and had rituals and ceremonies to honor it. They revered mountains and hills because they were thought to be physical representations of powerful spirits, and they gave offerings to them to please these deities. One of the most ancient tribes, the Puebloans, believed that their gods lived inside the earth, and they dedicated entire buildings called kivas to the spirits dwelling within. In some geographical regions of the United States, it is still common practice to carve a ceremonial hole in the ground and plant corn kernels as a tribute to the earth.

Best Tips and Tricks to Spot the Best Rocks/Gems/Minerals Etc

Do we have the right to collect gems? Searching gems and fossils with a few basic tips will not be too complicated. It is also vital to know that there is extensive regulation in this regard to ensure personal safety and increase the chances of success of the extraction.

Collecting Precious Stones: The Regulations

It is the first thing that we must clear before starting any search for precious stones. To what extent do we have the right to collect and keep gems for our private collection?

You must pay attention and know what is possible and what is not. Not everything is allowed!

Suppose your parents or grandparents told you beautiful stories about the stones and precious metals they collected in their time. In that case, it is better to know that the legislation has changed a lot and is increasingly restrictive regarding the collection and extraction of minerals.

First advice regarding the collection of gemstones:

- No unauthorized removal! Indeed, we cannot collect stones without authorization from a privately owned site, a mining operation, or a working quarry.
- Although these sites are, in many cases, outdoors and easily accessible, entering requires authorization.
- Even if you have permission to collect stones or fossils on private land, that does not mean everything is automatically in order.

For example, if the land is located in another country, you will be subject to the restrictions dictated by the state and customs since everything you find will have to be declared.

Second advice regarding the extraction of precious stones:

- Certain alpine regions authorize the collection of gems and metals on payment of a permit. You can find famous mining regions in Austria, Switzerland, and Italy. The extraction must be carried out using a hammer and burin. Forage machines and explosives such as dynamite are reserved for professionals and the region's inhabitants.

The third tip for collecting gems and fossils:

- National parks and protected natural areas systematically prohibit the collection of minerals and vegetables. We have all found, at least once in our lives, a heart-shaped gem on a walk along a river or in the mountains. Attention, in a national park, collecting a gem will have the same weight as collecting precious stones or fossils.
- It is only possible if you participate in an activity organized by a geology club or the national park itself. Logically you will find all the information about it on the Internet.

Take a Druse or Geode?

Gemologists and mineralogists use the term druse. A druse is a gem full of crystals that requires several months, even years of research.

In the Alps, a geode filled with crystals must be marked to warn that it has been discovered by someone who will return to study it or extract the crystals.

Since 1970 a druse can be retained for study for two years. Anyone who does not respect this retention time will be charged with theft.

How Do You Identify a Natural Stone?

Natural stones that are usually translucent such as quartz, fluorite, amethyst, or prehnite, are easy to identify because they do not have a uniform color, and depending on the angle from which we look at them, they can be darker or lighter. On the contrary, a stone that is not natural does not have translucent areas, and the color does not vary.

The color changes and saturation depend solely and exclusively on the temperature at which the stones are found and their chemical components, so it is impossible to find an artificial stone equal to a natural one.

However, there are other more opaque stones, such as aventurine, opal, or amazonite, whose imitations can lead to doubts if we do not analyze them closely. In both cases, the color is usually uniform and has the same saturation.

To differentiate them, our best advice is to pay attention to the brightness and veining. The natural shine is infinitely more elegant than the artificial one, and an opaque natural stone usually has veins of other shades. In addition, listening to the sound produced when two stones collide with each other helps us confirm whether it is a natural stone.

Tips For Collecting Minerals

Collecting minerals implies acquiring basic knowledge to learn to recognize them, which is achieved by reading guides and related books, following the advice of expert collectors, visiting museums, monographic fairs, markets, and exchange tables, in specialized stores, and, of course, online.

The collector will soon know how to distinguish a mineral from a rock, classify them in their class (elements, sulfides, halides, oxides, carbonates, sulfates, phosphates, silicates, and organics), their main properties: most common color, shine (metallic, greasy, vitreous, etc.), exfoliation, fracture, hardness, density, the most frequent crystalline habits (whether they form aggregates or twins, geodes, druses), their paragenesis, minerals that have formed together under the same conditions,

Tip to Start the Mineral Collection

1. Generic mineral guides are useful to consult anywhere, although the photos they usually show are rarely representative; thus, we can observe wonderful unusual specimens or enlarged microscopic samples that we hope to find later in large sizes and at a good price.
2. The Internet can be a magnificent resource, but the abundance of pages consulted can lead to disorientation in the search for a specific aspect. Choose the most trusted sources.
3. Attendance at museums and fairs is highly recommended, giving an exact idea of what we see on the different web pages.
4. If in doubt, consult dealers or other more advanced collectors.

Search And Acquisition of Minerals

- There are several ways to obtain minerals. Through our collection, visiting sites (deposits, mine dumps) where we can find the specimens. Over time, a good "local" collection can be built up.
- By gift or exchanging samples with other collectors.
- Buying them at mineral fairs or specialized stores. In this way, we can access other methods' hard-to-obtain copies.

How to Acquire Minerals for The Collection

At the beginning of the collection, it is usual and logical to be not very selective and not have very defined criteria. We will find many interesting specimens reasonably priced, usually in 4×4 cm boxes. Or also something bigger that catches our attention (brightly colored, shiny, transparent, etc.).

Little by little, we will be looking at minerals of the highest level; here, it is necessary to comment that there are no two identical samples; a small difference marks the different prices (size, shape, more or less perfect crystals, origin of the sample and state of conservation and presentation).

The conditioning factor of the price is obvious, we limit ourselves to what is within our monetary possibilities or the limit of what we want to spend, but as a general rule, for the good future development of your collection, if you have to choose, it is always better to buy a good copy than two or three of inferior quality. The experience and many copies make you know if the purchase is good.

Advanced Mineral Collection Criteria

To select a mineral specimen for your collection and discard a similar one of the same or another species, the selection criteria are:

- Size of the piece or crystals.
- Minerals are included "in the matrix," with the latter proportional to the size of the crystals.
- Nice arrangement of crystals, associations, and druses in the general set of the piece.
- General aesthetics: color, transparency, brightness.
- Conservation: if it lacks breakages, blows, or defects typical of the sample.
- Labeled. The mineral must be labeled as completely as possible, including the locality.

Advice for Advanced Collectors

1. At the time of purchase, you can have a small guide handy to consult.
2. Make a list of what you have and want, and take it with you when you go mineral shopping.

3. Carry a 10x hand loupe to look at the smallest minerals or any detail in the big ones.
4. Ask the seller for the label of the copy purchased.
5. Do not touch the exposed parts without permission; if so, be careful. Sometimes we can find very brittle minerals.

Where to Look in The Fields

Semi-Precious Stones in Road Cuts

Rock hunting can be a rewarding hobby. A person can derive great satisfaction from a "great find," and many precious, semi-precious stones and minerals are found on public or private land. Sometimes you have to look down to find interesting rocks, but there are a wide variety of places where nature or man has helped uncover these "buried treasures." For example, road surfaces are sometimes built through hills and mountains using heavy machinery. These excavations often expose multiple layers of soil and minerals buried within.

- STEP
  1

Find a suitable road cut that is accessible and known to contain the rocks or minerals you are looking for. An excellent method to do this is to use a copy, if one exists, of a geological survey map of the area, along with a local road map. Another, and certainly easier, is an online search to see what rock-finding friendly roadblocks are in your area. Become familiar with the types of rocks and formations in which the gems and minerals you want are likely to be found.

- STEP
  2

Stand well back from the road when you reach the roadblock. Park your vehicle, so it does not obstruct traffic or the view of passing drivers. Look for exposed rocks and formations likely to contain the stones you are looking for. You can use the ladder if you decide to dig in higher places.

- STEP
  3

Use a rock hammer and cold chisel to expose more places gradually. Examine the rock you break for traces of semi-precious stones. Use a paintbrush when necessary to remove rock dust or sand. Carefully remove all surrounding rock samples, taking care to cause as little damage to the specimen as possible. Use the field guide to help you identify anything you find.

- STEP
  4

Put any discoveries you make in plastic bags. Mark on your map all the details that will help you locate the same place again in the future. Thoroughly clean when you're done to leave the area as it was when you found it.

Where To Look for Minerals

As we have said, many collectors start with a random collection of rocks, minerals, and fossils. As the collection grows, they take other criteria and become more selective in looking for thematic collections. One of the ways to acquire them quickly is in mineral stores, both physical and online. But, it must be said that it is more interesting and entertaining to be the one who finds and collects them. Many places offer guides to the best directions to find rocks, minerals, and fossils.

Although it should be noted that the collection of minerals presents some problems and limitations: mines with restricted access, dangerous old mines, depleted dumps, and some mines are on private property.

However, it should be noted that traditional collecting sites, such as road cuts and eroded coastal cliffs, remain excellent sites offering good opportunities to find good minerals. You will have to go with a good mineral search team to find good minerals.

Safety And Code of Ethics

Collecting minerals isn't going to hurt anyone unless you're reckless. The first warning is that you should never enter an old mine for several reasons: one is that there is almost no ore left because it has already been extracted. The other is that the underpinnings may be rotten, and everything may collapse. A good place could be the dumps, but you must be careful because they can be unstable.

If you are looking for minerals in cliffs, road cuts, or fallen rocks, be careful not to step on the wrong foot and that nothing falls from above.

Identification Of Minerals

We will discuss indicators easily recognizable by both beginner and experienced mineral collectors. It must be said that the physical properties are determined by the crystalline structure and the chemical composition of the mineral.

Color

Some minerals can have characteristic colors that make their identification easy: the vivid blue of azurite, the yellow of sulfur, or the green of malachite are some examples. On the other hand, others, such as fluorite, can be found in all colors, so its other properties must identify it.

The color in minerals is given by their absorption or the refraction of light at certain frequencies. One of the causes is trace elements or atoms that are not part of the basic chemical composition. The mineral's color can also be due to the lack of an atom or an ionic radical. Finally, the color of a mineral can be produced by the flawless structure itself, which can refract light in a certain way.

Stripe Color

As you have read, the color can be determined by impurities such as the mineral, but what is always unique and invariant is the color of the stripe. This can be easily seen by rubbing a corner of the mineral sample on a porcelain plate.

Brightness

The luster of a mineral states how the surface looks in reflected light. We can distinguish between metallic shine (they reflect light) and non-metallic shine (they do not reflect light). Minerals with metallic luster are usually opaque, and non-metallic minerals are usually transparent or translucent. Within these two, we find some subcategories of brightness: vitreous, adamantine, resinous, pearly, greasy, silky, matte, earthy, and metallic.

Exfoliation

Describes the ability of a mineral to break on flat, smooth surfaces. This is determined by the mineral's crystalline structure, in which the forces of attraction between atoms are weaker. Cleavage should be described by its direction relative to the crystal orientation and the ease with which it occurs. It can be said that perfect exfoliation generates smooth, soft, and shiny surfaces. A mineral can have perfect cleavage in one direction but not in another.

Fracture

Describes the ability of some minerals to break in directions other than the cleavage plans. The types of fractures that can occur are: hooked (with jagged edges), conchoidal (shell-like), smooth, unequal (irregularly rough), and splintered (with fibers in separate parts).

In addition, minerals can also be identified by their physical and chemical properties.

Where to Find Gems

If you are searching for gemstones in riverbeds and streams, it may take hours or even days to find anything. On the other hand, you could find many in a matter of minutes. The key to finding stones in the riverbed is knowledge of the geological processes that create and transport them. Roaming the desert and starting dredging or panning for gems is not legal. Check with local authorities before leaving.

Process

All gems are formed by slow cooling and crystallization in the earth's crust. As crystallized rock is exposed due to weathering processes, pieces break off. These pieces are carried in the mountains by streams and rivers. Finally, when the stream's current is no longer strong enough to carry these jewels, they are deposited in the stream beds. Days, weeks, or hundreds of years later, you can find these treasures beneath the shallows.

River Bed Searches

When you search the riverbeds, you are just as capable of finding a gold nugget, a historical artifact, as precious stones. For the best chance of finding the gems, find a location downstream from a gemstone mine or a location already known to be a productive location. The spots to find more gems arise in riverbeds when the current is too weak to carry heavy objects. Piles of sediment and stones show that a river has a history of depositing material there. The most common places where heavy objects such as gold and precious stones are deposited are the lowest points of a river and where the river curves.

Common Gems

The type of gems you find will depend on where you find them. Different gems form over thousands of years due to specific geological conditions, such as pressure and heat. Idaho, the "gem state," is the nation's second-largest garnet producer; these gems are often found by searching the river. Opals and rubies are other gems frequently found in Idaho. North Carolina is another nation's top gem-hunting spot for treasure hunting. In addition to garnets and rubies, the riverbeds of North Carolina have been known to bear sapphires and emeralds.

Any mineral or gemstone that forms due to geological processes can be found in stream beds. Quartz is the most famous crystal on earth and is often found in streams. It is common to find amethyst, jasper, topaz, and beryl in stream beds.

Considerations

Searching riverbeds and alluvial deposits for gemstones can severely damage a river's ecosystem. It involves using a suction cup to remove sediment and small rock deposits from stream beds. If you remove too much, the stream banks could collapse, and the ground around them could become too loose to support life. Always contact a local geological organization to determine where gem hunting is legal. For example, the Department of Lands oversees the state's open pit, public gem mines, and riverbeds and lakes. Strict regulations related to the dredging and surface mining of these areas.

How To Hunt for Gems

Gemstones are true treasures that have fascinated people for centuries. However, the visions some may have of workers diligently working in deep mines with jewel crystals are far from reality. You can find precious stones. The United States has many places that are potential sources of gemstones. Hunting for them can be as easy as driving to a mine that is open to the public or as difficult as getting your hands on geological information and discovering your existing location.

On The Hunt for Precious Stones

Instructions:

- Locate known sites where gemstones have been found in the past. Diamond State Park in Arkansas and the ruby mines of Franklin, North Carolina, are good examples.
- Investigation of the geology and geochemistry of gemstones to better understand where and in what rock conditions you might find them if you want to make your finds.
- Study the type of jewel you want to find. Learn to identify stone in its raw, uncut state. Many uncut gemstones look plain and dull compared to when they are cut.
- Obtain and use the proper tools. Shovels, buckets, and screens are all useful for hunting jewelry.
- Use a shovel to dig out gem-bearing soil or a pick to matrix the gem-bearing rock from a deposit or suspect and place them in a bucket. Take the bucket from a nearby water source.
- Pour a portion of the bucket into a screen and pour water over the material to clean up dirt, mud, and other debris.
- Look over large rocks and remove any that are not jewels or do not contain gems. Use a rock hammer to break bigger rocks to search for hidden treasures. Continue working through the material, removing any medium rocks. Comb through the smaller rocks for gem crystals.
- Keep an eye out for crystals that may just be exposed on the surface around the tank. Many valuable stones have been found in this way.
- Try a mine dump if you have permission to do so and can afford the equipment.

Do's And Don'ts of Rockhounding

When you begin to explore the universe of rocks, minerals, gems, and crystals, you may not know what you might learn or discover. You can specialize in rock types, like agates or geodes, or focus on metallic minerals, like gold.

Either way, you're guaranteed to discover new treasures, meet new people, and find something to learn new things about every day.

Make sure you record where each stone or fossil is found. You'll know precisely where to look if you ever encounter it again (often). Also, having your collection helps others who may have lost their quarry. If they happen upon one of your rocks, they might recognize them by the information written down and tell you where theirs ended up.

Rockhounding can be an expensive hobby. If you want to get the best value for your money, here are some tips:

- Buy only high-quality specimens;
- Do not buy anything just because you like its color or shape. Your love for it should never influence your decision-making process. Only purchase stones or fossils based on how valuable they are (i.e., rare finds);
- Look for deals whenever possible (i.e., when rockhounds are selling off their collections, there's bound to be something good somewhere).

You now understand why it is so important to collect the best materials. However, even though many think rockhounding is easy to work, it is quite hard. It requires skill and expertise to find the best specimens, which means you must acquire knowledge.

Here are few interesting tips to help you become a successful rockhound:

- Never rush. Even though you're excited about finding something, remember that patience is key. Rockhounding takes time and effort. Go slowly and perform thorough research of the site, take your time, and follow your instincts;
- Learn from experience. The best way to learn how to be a successful rockhound is to read books and articles about the subject;
- Don't assume. Sometimes rocks may seem similar but are very different after closer inspection. Remember that every rock has unique features (i.e., color, texture, shape, etc.). Make sure you study them carefully;
- Take notes. Record the location of each specimen that you find. You never know when you might lose track of where you last saw something;
- Always carry a camera. Taking pictures of your discoveries helps you remember where you found them and makes it easier for you to share your findings with other rockhounds.
- Dress properly. Wear comfortable clothing and sturdy shoes when rockhounding. In addition, make sure to wear sunscreen and bring water as well.

Book 6 Make Money with Rocks

How to Sell a Rock Collection

If you have a rock collection that you want to sell, there are many ways to go about it. Rock collectors connect through various outlets, whether trade shows, eBay, or a dealer. Knowing the details of your collection and staying current on hot-selling pieces can increase your chances of making a competitive profit.

Instructions

Increase the Value of Your Rock Collection

- Maintain the natural appearance of the rocks. Limiting exposure to artificial light and cleaning rocks using simple household materials such as alcohol can protect your investment and increase the likelihood of future earnings.

- Establish an organized system. If you plan to sell a rock collection, buyers are more attracted to collections with detailed records, labels, and complete information regarding the acquisition of each piece.

- Learn the names of the rocks in your collection. Savvy buyers may prefer to deal with a knowledgeable seller about the different types of Calcite or marble, for example.

  - Sale of stones from the best locations. For example, tourmaline from California is much more valuable than comparable tourmaline from Brazil or Connecticut.

Download the Rock Collection

- Change it! You can avoid spending on a new one, as most rock collectors enjoy a good trade now and then.
- Internet publicity. Popular websites like eBay can help you post your color photo collection and set minimum bidding for the sale of your merchandise.
- Contact a geology or natural history museum, especially if you are a collector of rare stones. Museums are often interested in hard-to-find pieces not generally available to the public.
- Consider selling the collection in parts or its entirety. Some prospective buyers opt for individual pieces, such as certain types of crystal, in a collection rather than buying the whole group.
- Work with a distributor. Some operate exclusively online, while others operate in person. Many dealers buy rock collections without seeing the collection, especially if you have desirable pieces.
- Be prepared to answer questions. Buyers often have many questions, including price, shipping, sample, account size, who's worked, and the historical value and status of the screen, to name just a few.

Gemstones, also called gems, are particular minerals or rocks used in jewelry making. They have peculirarities that make them attractive for personal adornments or jewelry decoration.

Gems are categorized as precious and semi-precious stones based on their beauty and hardness. A difference you should consider if you think about selling precious stones that you have. The most valuable and the only ones considered precious are the diamond, the ruby, the sapphire, and the emerald. However, other semi-precious stones have value, such as amethyst, topaz, pearl, zircon, and spinel.

What Gemstones Are Most Valued When Selling?

All gemstones are considered high-value items. So much so that in the past, they served as currency, and only nobles and royalty had access to them.

However, when selling precious stones, one stands out above the rest. We are talking about the diamond.

Diamond comprises carbon atoms arranged in a very stable cubic crystal structure. Its qualities include being the hardest mineral in the world and one of the brightest gemstones on the planet. These characteristics, together with their scarcity, make selling diamonds an excellent resource to obtain quick money.

How to Know the Value of a Diamond?

When it comes to selling diamonds, emeralds, rubies, sapphires, amethysts, or any type of precious stone, it is vital to know the market price. For this, four main factors are taken into account:

- Purity is one of the main indicators that must be considered when selling precious stones. This quality refers to the number of inclusions of small impurities. The fewer impurities, the higher the value.
- Size By this, we mean the shape and quality of its proportions. The cleaner the diamond or other gemstone is cut, the more value it will have.
- Color is the hue of the gemstone. Not all are the same, and the price varies depending on their rarity.
- Weight, The weight of gems such as diamonds also influences their valuation. It is expressed in carats. The more carats, the higher the value.

Jewelry made from natural stones is not only an accessory but also a profitable investment, but only if it is jewelry made of precious metals with natural stones. It is worth saying that not only diamonds are precious, and the range of natural stones is simply huge, but it is important to know how to assess their quality, not fall for a fake correctly, and, most importantly, what parameters determine the cost of stones.

What are gems? Natural minerals are considered precious, mostly of a crystalline nature, which has no color or a beautiful, uniform color of moderate tone, transparency, hardness, brilliance, play in the light and cause admiration. A natural gemstone must be resistant to wear and fading and an external chemical attack.

Natural stones are used to create jewelry and other artistic products, and their price is largely determined by the abundance of the gem in natural conditions. There are several opposing classifications of gemstones, the most common of which are jewelry and general (considering the cost of gems).

Jewelry masters divide all stones into natural and synthetic. Artificial gems have no material value, but natural ones can be of organic or mineral origin and are divided into several categories.

In jewelry and trade, all natural stones are divided into precious, semi-precious, and ornamental. Among the precious stones are rocks of mineral origin with high hardness and transparency - diamonds, emeralds, sapphires, rubies, and natural organic pearls. The size of a crystal and its value are determined by its carat weight. A diamond is a hardest and most expensive gemstone obtained by cutting a diamond. The cost of diamonds, in addition to size, is also determined by their color and clarity (the Presence of natural defects). Precious stones, names, and photos found in the book can be selected in appearance and terms of quality characteristics, and other parameters.

Emerald is a rather fragile and opaque stone, which is valuable, first of all, for its unusual green color, a shade of fresh grass.

- Ruby - one of the subspecies of the mineral origin of the corundum stone, has a bright and rich red color.
- Sapphire is also part of the corundum group, has high transparency, and its shades range between dark blue and pale blue. In nature, sapphires are quite rare. However, their cost is lower than that of rubies.
- Pearls are precious stones of organic origin, formed in the shells of sea and river mollusks. The color of the pearls is from white to black. The larger the pearl grain, the higher its value. Semi-precious stones can also be transparent or colored, and among them, the most popular are turquoise; pomegranate, topaz; amethyst; tourmaline; zircon; opal, quartz, and spinel.
- Ornamental stones are slightly transparent or generally opaque minerals of low hardness. At the same time, these stones are distinguished by a beautiful natural pattern and color, which is why they are extensively used in jewelry.
- The most common gemstones are cornelian, agate; onyx; cat's eye; jasper, and malachite. The abundance of classifications of precious stones is because experts from different fields distinguish different qualitative characteristics of gems necessary for their business and divide stones into types following such characteristics.

There are classifications based on:

- the chemical composition of crystals,
- the origin of the stones,
- sizes;
- flowers;
- crystallographic parameters;
- processing methods,
- cost;
- medicinal properties,
- purpose.

The German scientist Kluge formed the first science-based classification demonstrating which stones are precious was formed in 1860, which divided stones into precious and semi-precious and different classes according to their physical characteristics. Subsequently, knowledge about stones increased, and the classification was supplemented. The simplest and most accurate is the division of stones into groups according to their purpose: jewelry, and ornamental.

To date, the most complete and widespread is the classification of gems by the scientist Kievlenko, which considers both the purpose and the cost of precious stones. According to this classification, gems are divided into groups and orders within these groups:

- Jewelry
  stones

  - 1st order: diamond, ruby, emerald, blue sapphires.
  - 2nd order: orange alexandrite, purple and green sapphires, black opals, jadeite.
  - 3rd order: spinel, fire and white opals, topazes, aquamarine, tourmaline, rhodolite.

- 4th order: chrysolite, zircon, beryl, turquoise, amethyst, citrine.

- Jewelry and ornamental stones

  - 1st order: lapis lazuli, jade, malachite, charoite, amber, rock crystal.
  - 2nd order: agate, hematite, obsidian. ornamental stones jasper; onyx; pegmatite; quartzite. gemstone colors

Run a Business Selling Rocks/Minerals/Gems

A gem or precious stone is a precious or semi-precious mineral that can be cut with specific tools for jewelry or other crafts. A precious or semi-precious stone can refer to certain rocks, such as lapis lazuli, or organic materials, such as amber, similar to gems. There are many ways to enter this market. Rough and uncut gems or stones may be imported directly from their origin countries or purchased from wholesale distributors. In addition, gems and polished stones can be purchased for sale through a retail store or mail order from jewelry manufacturers or other artisans.

Conduct Industry Research

Learn about the different types of gems and precious and semi-precious stones. Learn to identify quality, both in rough and cut gemstones. Gain insight into market values, which often fluctuate based on supply. For example, some gems require certification from organizations such as the Gemological Institute of America (GIA).

Make a business plan. This will help you determine the venture's feasibility, identify its objectives and determine the financial and human capital requirements. The US Small Business Administration offers help writing this plan with online resources.

Start the business identity procedures. Apply for a tax identification number (TIN) with the IRS and set up a business bank account for the new entity.

Set the company address. This business can be operated with a special electronic address for companies through a printed catalog and a professional website. In this case, an email address will suffice. To sell directly to the public in a retail setting, lease a store.

Selecting the business community is one of the most important steps in starting a new business. Access to vehicular and pedestrian traffic is an important consideration.

Join industry organizations. The American Gem Trade Association (AGTA) is a professional organization that offers its members access to industry publications, such as the AGTA Source Directory. They also organize the annual fair, which attracts wholesalers and gemstone dealers. The Tucson Gem and Mineral Society (TGMS) also produces a major annual fair. This attracts the industry's top distributors, wholesalers, retailers, jewelry makers, and other artisans.

Social Media to Sell Rocks

It seems unbelievable, but it is becoming increasingly difficult to survive day to day without accessing a social network: Facebook, Twitter, Instagram, Pinterest, WhatsApp, or LinkedIn are just a few examples of these simple means of communication and interaction between people that, in a way, constantly guide human behavior. The economic and social changes that have arisen in recent decades and the emergence of new information and communication technologies have become an uprising of small (and not so small) things, making it impossible to understand everyday life without taking a look at the Smartphone, looking for comments on social networks, some interesting hashtag or photos and videos of virtual friends.

In reality, social networks are not only used for this type of activity: in recent times, these systems have managed to transform themselves into enormous electronic commerce platforms, full of potential consumers who access, share interests and provide very valuable information daily. Their tastes become a very interesting tool for advertisers of certain products. This confirms the interest of retailers and wholesalers in focusing their marketing strategies on social networks, where a Like or a Retweet can be transformed into the sale of a product or a service. The future has arrived as a social network, becoming a success for buying and selling in all commercial sectors, especially with the possibility of using mobile accounts to access them.

To date, companies have used more traditional marketing strategies, characterized by other mechanisms to make themselves known: mass and specialized advertising in non-digital media, physical mail, attendance at trade fairs, merchandising sales, public relations, or expensive advertising. To face, among many other possibilities. In reality, these strategies also had their positive side. In addition to the reach of some magazines or physical advertising media, face-to-face contact is capable of generating the necessary credibility to convert an interested party into a client. Likewise, these more traditional strategies allow reaching sectors of the population that, with great difficulty, could have access to new technologies, as is the case of the elderly,

Even so, and according to studies, around 14% of current consumers have bought at some time through a social network, and 65% of social network users acknowledge that their purchases have been influenced, on occasion, by the use of these platforms, in which the possibility of making purchases with a single click, after logging in, has already been inserted. The social network becomes, at this point, a vehicle capable of achieving many things.

In this sense, it is evident that the Natural Stone trade has also experienced strong innovation with the emergence of social networks as a new business tool. It is all about how to adapt to the new needs and demands of the consumer: after creating a web page full of appropriate colors, texts, and images, the online dissemination of a series of catalogs loaded with high-resolution images and Presence on social networks represents an interesting expansion of the range of customers since you never know the exact place where a potential customer can be found.

Online Jewelry Business

One of the great opportunities to sell your jewelry is through Social Networks, and in this BOOK, we will tell you how.

Nowadays, social networks are a fundamental part of our society. Thanks to them, we stay connected and are in constant communication, which is why a large part of the population's time is spent visiting them.

So you must know what each network on the web offers you.

1. Facebook

With Facebook, it is very functional since it can help you promote the launch of your products, deliver relevant content to your followers, open a channel to support customers, and even make sales.

Also, there are several options to increase the use of this network, and one of them is Facebook Ads, the advertising tool of this social network.

2. Instagram

Instagram is a dynamic and visual network, allowing you to interact with users in real time since they instantly see your products when you upload an image or video.

It also has its own ads tool, Instagram Ads, which is a great alternative for those who want to reach a larger audience.

3. Twitter

Twitter is another essential social network for those interested in interacting more quickly and briefly with the public.

In addition to tweets, you can also post photos, videos, and even links to external pages, allowing you to promote other communication channels or your sales page.

4. YouTube

YouTube is a Google video social network with more than a billion registered users. In addition, today, it is considered one of the most important search engines since many users use YouTube to search for various content.

With a YouTube channel, you can promote your products and become a reference in your niche since you can make videos that educate your audience and help people solve small daily problems related to your area of action.

Now that you know the process, you can take advantage of each of the networks you can use, and it is time to know how you can boost your sales on social networks.

1. Define objectives

It is important to define the goals you want to have once you use social networks to promote your brand, and a simple way to define them is by asking the following questions:

- Why do we want to be on social networks?
- How can we measure our goals?
- Are they specific objectives?
- Who do I want to reach?
- How do I want to be known?

Once you avail the answers to these questions, you will have to consider that social networks are not like traditional media since, thanks to them, we can have bilateral channels of communication, which means that you will have an almost immediate response to everything you give. To know, so that will help you grow and get to know your audience better.

2. Define your target audience

The second step is to carry out research to identify our target audience, for which it is important to listen to users, for example, their different opinions about the products, criticisms about them, content that particularly interests them, among other opinions, and understand the context in which they find themselves when they see us.

3. Select the Content

Do you have to do this point thinking about how to catch my customers? Well, the answer is that you have to create content of interest to them, which means you have to seek to make various publications and leave your users learning.

Something you have to keep in mind is that your users see you as an expert on the subject of jewelry, so you have to give recommendations, examples, advice, and more; in this way, your clients, in addition to following you for your wonderful designs, they will also follow you for the knowledge you bring them.

Also, try to create eye-catching and very visual content, as we have discussed how each social network works; this is a very important point, so you have to be aware of the composition of your images and videos going to go up.

Seek that all your pieces look their best and that they look like the wonderful designs they are to impress those who visit your networks.

4. Offer excellent customer service

We cannot leave this point behind because this is where you are going to have much more personal and close contact with your clients, so it is vital to respond quickly and do it through the same channel in which you contacted us; this will help you drive your customers and persuade them to make a safer purchase.

5. Product photography

They say that "love is born from sight," which is true. When we enter a store, the first thing we see attractive catches our attention, and we buy it almost without thinking. The same happens in social networks and digital media in general. Try to take some good photos of your products and items, with the details defined so that customers can see them. Even if you aren't a skilled photographer or have the best equipment, the creativity and a camera that gives you good effects will suffice.

Don't think about it anymore and take advantage of your social networks to show everyone your incredible designs, but above all, increase those sales through one of the most used channels today.

Selling Jewelry Online, Is It Profitable?

It is an excellent time to open your business online, and what better way to do it than with one of the fastest growing industries in the world: jewelry.

Today is an excellent time to open your own online business, and what better way to do it than with one of the fastest growing industries in the world: jewelry.

Whether you offer jewelry boxes to fine pieces of precious metals, it is important to define a couple of points before launching into the adventure of undertaking on the Internet.

Selling jewelry can be a good way to start a business and enter e-commerce.

We want to tell you that it doesn't matter if you already have a physical store or want to start completely online; having a virtual store is essential in today's jewelry market.

However, it cannot be easy to get started. If this is your plan, we are sure that doubts like these will arise in your mind:

- Is it reliable to sell online?
- How do I open an online store?
- Is it necessary to leap to the digital world, or can I keep my store? Traditional?
- To solve them, you can consult this note, where we address why it is important to sell online.

The Big Picture of Jewelry in Business

Jewelry is a multi-billion dollar market globally. In a way that it does not matter if you are an artist who designs your pieces, distributes leather jewelry boxes, costume jewelry, fine jewelry, or just wants to start your brand, you can make good profits.

As it is a consumer product, this business has no limits, as it is attractive to men and women of any age, social status, or culture. There are rings, necklaces, bracelets, anklets, piercings, and watches, and as if that were not enough, each of these products can be made from your precious mineral/rock and gem collection, such as gold, silver, diamonds, precious stones, and many more.

The jewels are so diverse that if you start to investigate the multitude of options, you will not find an end; there is everything! And that is where the valuable opportunity to open your business lies: a hallmark, something that makes you different from the rest, unique.

Since fashion is a volatile industry, you'll need to keep things interesting by updating your product range and adding up-to-date trends. Keep in mind that fashion is a rapidly evolving niche.

Advantages of Selling Jewelry Online

The advantages of Internet commerce apply equally to any product or service, but in the particular case of jewelry, three points stand out:

- Shipping: The jewelry does not take up a lot of space and is light, making it an excellent shipping product. Because they require little packaging, shipping costs will be low.
- Sizes: selling jewelry online has an important advantage. Unlike clothing, most people don't need to try on jewelry to know if it fits or not. Of course, there are exceptions, such as rings, but it is a very small niche that does not have major complications.
- Variety: There is a wide variety of jewelry with a wide range of prices. As we mentioned, jewelry's universe is almost infinite, from materials to designs.

Selling Jewelry Online: How Do I Start?

If you have already decided to start your digital business selling jewelry, jewelry boxes, or any other related product, pay attention to the first steps you must follow to start your project:

1. Identify the type of jewelry you want to sell

Without a doubt, this is the first aspect to consider. Take the time to identify and define what type of jewelry you want to sell. There are the following categories:

- Fine jewelry is made with metals and precious stones such as diamonds and sapphires. The high quality of the materials stands out over the design or the manufacturing technique. Although the prices will be quite high, they mean higher profits when you make a sale.
- Handmade jewelry. Handmade jewelry stands out for its artistic style. Semi-precious stones and unusual materials like bone are often used to create one-of-a-kind pieces. Customers are attracted by that feature and not so much by the material.
- Costume jewelry: This type of jewelry is more affordable, fashionable, produced in larger quantities, and made from inexpensive materials. While prices are lower, you'll have to sell a lot to profit.
- Vintage Jewelry: Antique jewelry and jewelry boxes have become an increasingly popular option. Some people enjoy treasure hunting, so vintage jewelry provides an opportunity to purchase something unique and storied.

2. Define your market niche

The jewelry market is very diverse. Men do not usually look the same as women, just as age influences them. While some people associate the word jewel with luxury, others prefer antique treasures. Most people cannot afford the cost of diamonds and prefer jewelry pieces, while for others, gemstones are synonymous with engagement rings.

3. Develop your brand

Now that you have defined the type of jewelry and niche, you are ready to create your brand. We know that marketing can be a bit overwhelming at first, so don't hesitate to hire experts who know how to translate your ideas and design everything you need to start your online business: from your store name, logo, and slogan to your website and social networks.

How to Stand Out on The Internet with Your Jewelry Line
On the Internet and social networks, many accounts are dedicated to this, you may not be discovering the black thread by venturing to do it, but if there is a wide offer, it is because many people want it. So it doesn't mean you don't have chances to get noticed as a new store.

A good platform to stand out is Instagram; you can stand out using the publications of your competition. But several secrets or even necessary rules will help you win a new audience.

You must understand that when you sell a product like jewelry, the important thing is the visual, and Instagram is the right space. So to sell jewelry, you need to be very creative because if you don't do it right, your products could seem cheaper than they are.

1. Use coupons, gifts, and sales

Since there are already a lot of stores selling jewelry on Instagram, it can be a challenge to stand out when you have just created a new account; a good way to attract potential customers is through coupons, discounts, special offers, and giveaways through your account or with vloggers, influencers and more.

One of the most popular techniques now used by new stores is to reach numerous micro-influencers. No need to contact top bloggers who never or hardly ever check your direct messages. Connecting with simple users who have between 1K and 5K of the audience can give you more results; the most important thing is that the style of their accounts matches your brand identity.

The exchange happens like this: you give away some jewelry pieces and receive photos of the characters you can use in your profile. Also, Instagram algorithms like your account to be frequently tagged and mentioned; therefore, your posts will show up more often on Explore and to the followers of these micro-influencers.

2. Stand out from your competition in your biography

Remember that the bio (or biography) is the first piece of information potential customers see at a glance. They can't immediately see the text of your posts, so the bio is the main caption that makes an impression.

The good idea is to write in 150 characters the meaning, value, and competitive advantage. Explain why your store provides more value than the competition and what is special about it.

3. Be responsive and active in messages

One problem that many stores, including perhaps your competitors, have is that they take a long time or do not respond to Direct messages on Instagram. Some may even mention in their bio that customers should not contact them via DM.

Private messages on Instagram can be where you connect most deeply with your audience; using direct messages will help build loyalty, especially if your brand is new to the market.

Repeated sales through Instagram usually happen if buyers are satisfied: they are the ones who become loyal to the brand. You have to connect with them after the sale. So that's where you can take advantage to close the sale, and if you don't have an online store, you can use Remote Payments so that the transaction happens at that moment.

4. Take good care of how your photos look

As we said, jewelry is a delicate product requiring a brilliant Instagram presentation. You can't just put your products on a table to take unclear photos: it won't arouse anyone's admiration. Regardless of how beautiful and unique your products are, no one will consider ordering if the visuals are poor.

First, poor visual effects lower the level of trust in the store, especially if something precious and expensive is being sold. Second, high-quality and creative visuals allow you to play around with pricing. Even when your product is of the same or even lower quality than competitors, the price can be substantially higher just because of a great Instagram account.

The bottom line is that people buy a complete image that includes a photo or a video through Instagram. It is no longer just a physical product that they want. Through the visual, a person perceives the product.

SME Marketing: How to Sell a Stone?

In SME Marketing, it is extremely important to have the labor, academic, and product knowledge to start and close a sale.

If you are an SME and you want to do Marketing to obtain the sales and profits established as your goals, let me write you the following tips so that you can sell even a stone :

1. You must detect your Resources, Skills, and Capacities as a good SME to be able to offer your market (customers) a stone that meets their needs. For example, in human resources; you must have trained and experienced salespeople to market your

products/services; in Skills and Capacities, your own sales staff have skills that help them sell faster; for example, they are friendly, bold, persuasive, patient, loyal, etc

2. Your sales force must know 100% of the product and service it offers to the market; here, I recommend doing a SWOT analysis (Strengths, Weaknesses, Opportunities, and Threats) to anticipate the possible client's objections. As a seller, I suggest you never lie to the customer about the benefits he will get if he buys our product or service!

3. The SME/Seller must believe in the product/service that it offers to the market 100%

4. We must study the direct and indirect competition to know their position in the market, the quality of the service and product, promotions, and feedback of their comments on their social networks.

5. Detect areas not covered by our competition in the market so that it is a business opportunity for our SME Marketing.

6. When facing the client, analyze their "non-verbal language" when offering our products/services.

7. Mention the benefits when purchasing our products/services.

8. Mention to the client (depending on the development of our negotiation) the promotions in force, which applies if they purchase our product and service today.

9. Be persuasive and not manipulative; many sellers get desperate in the development of the negotiation and resort to manipulation; I suggest that you be persuaded through the benefits of the product/service, the ease of obtaining credit, the complements of the product/service (post-sale, for example), sales

promotion, prestige/quality/reputation of the SME/brand/product/service.

10. Please provide the best service and customer care from the first visit to the last to gain their trust and liking for our brand/SMEs/products/services.

How to Make Money from a Blog

The cornerstone is your blog. The blog will allow you to be perceived as someone relevant and trustworthy.

It is about those people you are targeting being attracted to your content.

Let's not also talk about the fact that Google will start to position you in its search engine so you will gain visibility and notoriety.

There are different platforms to get started (WordPress, blogger), but I recommend hiring your domain and hosting for €45 a year and using WordPress.

From that moment, the key is perseverance. Publish at least one article of at least 500 words a week. Solve your potential client's real problems, add massive value, and those mid-market managers who love productivity apps will start following you. Good! And this is the beginning. By now, they know you. Surely after some time, they would be delighted to meet you in person, which would be a great opportunity to tell them about your products or services. This is social selling.

Your posts always have to have a call to action. You must, by all means, try to get the person who visits your posts to leave you their contact or email in exchange for some very good exclusive content or simply by subscribing to your newsletter.

After showing how to make money with a blog and seeing it as a great business, a clarification must be made. All the information is useless without two fundamental factors:

- quality content
- smart monetization strategies.

Just as progress in writing comes with practice, money comes from clever advertising strategies.

Today it is possible to make a blog a reliable source of income. A blog owner should not expect companies to contact them with sponsored content offers or blog banner ads to get enough clicks.

Made in United States
Troutdale, OR
12/20/2024

26932332R00124